Patterns and Instructions for
CARVING AUTHENTIC BIRDS

H. D. Green

Dover Publications, Inc.
New York

To Lorie, Leslie, and David

All carvings, photographs, and diagrams are by the author.

Published in Canada by General Publishing Company, Ltd., 30 Lesmill Road, Don Mills, Toronto, Ontario.
Published in the United Kingdom by Constable and Company, Ltd., 10 Orange Street, London WC2H 7EG.

Patterns and Instructions for Carving Authentic Birds is a new work, first published by Dover Publications, Inc., in 1982.

International Standard Book Number: 0-486-24222-6
Library of Congress Catalog Card Number: 81-68142

Manufactured in the United States of America
Dover Publications, Inc.
180 Varick Street
New York, N.Y. 10014

Contents

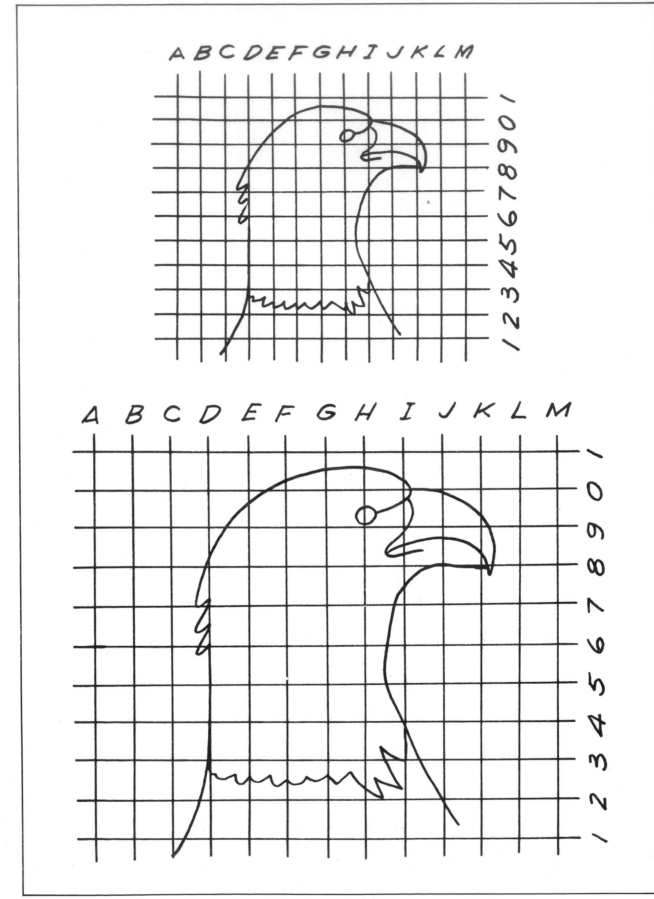

Illustration: Changing scale by the squares method.

Introduction

Creating likenesses of birds with wood and paint can be a most enjoyable leisure activity. Birds are everywhere; according to one conservative estimate, about one hundred billion of them inhabit the earth. To capture their various shapes and diverse plumage coloration accurately can be challenging and interesting.

My first book, *Carving Realistic Birds* (Dover 0-486-23484-3; 1977), was an attempt to share with others some of the enjoyment I have received over the years from this fascinating hobby. This second volume, though complete in itself, is intended to supplement the earlier book by providing additional carving patterns and photographs of the carvings made from these patterns. Purposely omitted are most of the step-by-step procedures for going from pattern to finished carving since these procedures were the primary subject of the earlier book. I have repeated a few of the procedures that I felt needed amplification, especially for the beginning carver, in addition to details that might require special attention. The patterns are a selection of the ones I have enjoyed using and, where possible, they have been drawn life size. Where this has not been

Figure 2. A Purple Martin in front of a bird house constructed especially for bird study.

possible, hash marks in the page margins will readily afford a change of scale by the squares method (see illustration).

It should be noted that, as in the earlier book, the patterns and carvings are presented here as

Figure 1. A Ruby-throated Hummingbird family hatches on a front porch.

Figure 3. A Clark's Nutcracker by a roadside.

carving aids and are but one carver's impression and interpretation of a particular species. Only a living bird is a true carving pattern. What the carver sees in the real bird and is able to manifest with his hands establishes the degree of realism that can be achieved. Good color photographs help to raise the degree of realism, but especially helpful is the study of birds in their natural environment. This can be accomplished in many ways, including the construction of houses and feeding stations, bird photography, and excursions to the shore or mountains or into the country. You will also experience an ever-increasing appreciation of the birds that can be seen in your own backyard and on the street or roadsides that you travel throughout the year.

I have put the carving projects in this book in the sequence in which the birds they are based on usually appear in good field guides. This sequence generally corresponds to the taxonomical categories devised to identify birds and to show each species' evolutionary relationships to other birds and animals. Within the class division Aves, to which all birds belong, taxonomists distinguish many orders. My part divisions—Shorebirds, Woodpeckers, Perching Birds, Gallinaceous Birds, and Raptors—correspond roughly to five principal orders of birds found in North America. These orders are Charadriiformes, Piciformes, Passeriformes, Galliformes, and Falconiformes. Perching Birds are heavily represented in this book to reflect their relative importance in the bird world: over half of the world's birds are Perching Birds. Current scientific names for the birds in every project are provided. I say "current" because ornithologists sometimes change birds' names in light of new zoological evidence, or to give credit to the discoverer of a particular species.

The personal satisfaction to be derived from carving realistic birds is considerable and one's enthusiasm is quick to grow. Waste no time regretting that you do not have the talent to carve them. Nature provides the basic materials and subject matter; you, like most of us, have the urge to create. Thus all the essentials for carving and painting a bird are available, and all that remains is for you to begin.

Figure 4.   A young Robin in a backyard.

I. Shorebirds

A variety of birds can be found near the shore, including sandpipers, plovers, gulls, terns, and auks. Patterns for Wilson's Plover and the Laughing Gull are provided herein. Most shorebirds are either white and gray or brown. Usually both sexes of a species are similarly colored.

While the patterns in this book have not been put in a sequence of carving complexity, the first two patterns are well suited for initial projects for the beginning carver. Each pattern contains only a small amount of feather definition and requires a minimum of carving time. In addition the construction options may be of value when the carver moves on to the remaining projects.

Wilson's Plover

Named for the nineteenth-century pioneer ornithologist Alexander Wilson, *Charadrius wilsonia* is distinguished within the plover family by its outsized bill. This feature has prompted the frequent use of the name "Thick-billed Plover." Like all plovers, Wilson's Plover nests in scantily lined depressions in the ground. It is perhaps best known for its "crippled bird act," which it puts on whenever an enemy or other

Figure 6. Wilson's Plover carving from above.

danger might be near. Its breeding range is from southern New Jersey to Texas. In fall many of the birds remain on the Gulf coast, but some head south to warmer winter climates.

Since the pattern indicates that the tail, wings, and beak should lie generally on parallel lines of grain, the carving can easily be constructed from a single block of wood. The only special care to be taken is when carving the tibiae, as these areas

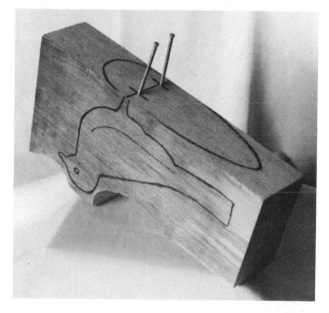

Figure 7. Temporarily inserting carving posts (finishing nails) into the tibiae to keep the wood from splitting during carving.

will be especially vulnerable to accidental breakage due to the nature of the wood grain. This problem can best be overcome by inserting carving posts (see Figure 7). Most plovers have only three visible toes. Feet may be constructed from wire and thread, as outlined in Diagram 18.

Use a pyroelectric pen (wood burner) to indi-

Figure 5. Wilson's Plover carving.

Figure 8.   *Most plovers have only three visible toes.*

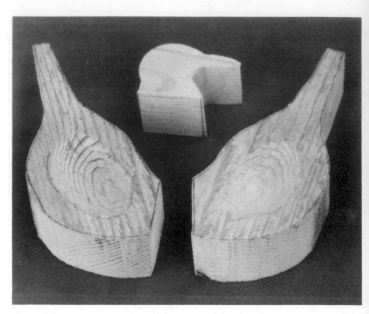

Figure 9.   *Laughing Gull head and body blocks. The body blocks have been hollowed out to prevent checking.*

cate feather barbs. With carving completed, paint the bill black, upper parts sandy, under parts white, and the feet and toes pinkish. Except for when it is young and during the winter, the male has a black patch on the crown and eyes and a black collar. The female lacks these black markings.

Laughing Gull

The Laughing Gull (*Larus atricilla*) derives its name from its call, an almost hysterical ha-ha-ha-haah-haah-haah. It is thought that its wine-red bill provides a means of communication between the adult and the newborn chick. The chick pecks at the red bill and the parent responds by regurgitating partially digested food for the offspring. When a properly colored model of a bill is placed near a chick, the chick will respond enthusiastically.

Laughing Gulls, like all other gulls, are short-legged, web-footed, and quite aquatic. Also like other gulls they are flying garbage disposals that eat just about everything: fruit, mice, wheat, grasshoppers, steak bones, eggs, fish, earthworms, and almost any trash left on beaches. In addition they can drink both fresh and salt water, as a pair of glands above their eyes removes the salt in seawater which is then excreted through openings in the bill.

Today there are forty-four recognized species of gulls, twenty-nine of which breed in the Western Hemisphere. Of these at least one species is to be found living part time in every state of the Union. Formerly the breeding range of the

Laughing Gull extended along the Atlantic and Gulf coasts from Maine to Texas, but habitat destruction and egg collecting have diminished the species' area. Since Laughing Gulls are so omnivorous, they perform a tremendous service to an ever-expanding and polluting human society.

The pattern portrays a bird with its head only slightly erect. This is particularly noteworthy since all gulls, especially young ones, must keep their necks tucked in. A raised head is an open invitation to battle.

Make the head and neck from a separate piece of stock. As shown on the pattern, the line of the grain should be parallel to the beak and joined to the body at the dashed line. Like other carvings in this book, the head may be positioned so that the bird will appear to be looking forward or to the side. Should the side position be desired, rotate the head at least fifteen degrees relative to the body's center line, since a smaller angle will make the completed carving look like it has an error. The body could be made from one piece of stock with the grain line running parallel to the wings and tail, but this would require a piece of stock approximately five inches thick that would be quite susceptible to cracking and checking because of its size. A better method is to construct the body from two pieces of wood glued together at the center line. Not only will the glue line act to prevent checking but the two halves when hollowed out as in Figure 9 make for a lighter block that will also be able to expand and contract better, as environmental conditions require.

Primary feathers can be carved from the body

Figure 10.   *Primary and tail feathers carved from the body block.*

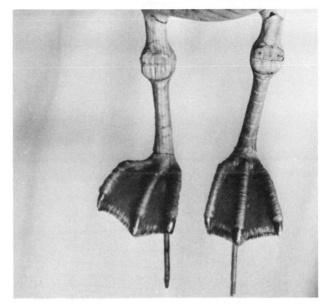

Figure 12.   *Feet for Laughing Gull.*

Figure 11.   *A stage in carving the Laughing Gull. A wooden dowel was used for the tibiae.*

block (see Figure 10). Another option is to make the primary feathers from separate pieces of thin stock that are then inserted into the body. The feet can be made by using a combination of wire, string, and wood, as described in Diagram 19. The procedure noted in Diagram 20 may also be used for gulls, especially when they are carved smaller than life size. When using the latter procedure for gulls, the hind toe should be modified to be just slightly visible on the back of the foot. In addition, webbing must be added to the bottom of the three front toes. The webbing can be made from wood veneer and bent as necessary to conform to the toes and the surface of the base.

Soak the veneer in water or steam it with a tea kettle to permit bending without splitting or breaking.

When the carving is completed, paint the bill and feet dusky red, the head and wing tips black, the ring around the eye and the rear wing edge white, the mantle dark gray, and the neck and underparts whitish. Winter birds have white heads with grayish markings, feet and bills also become more grayish. At the time of molting, young birds are brown with buff chins, white rumps, and black tail bands.

Figure 13.   *Completed Laughing Gull carving.*

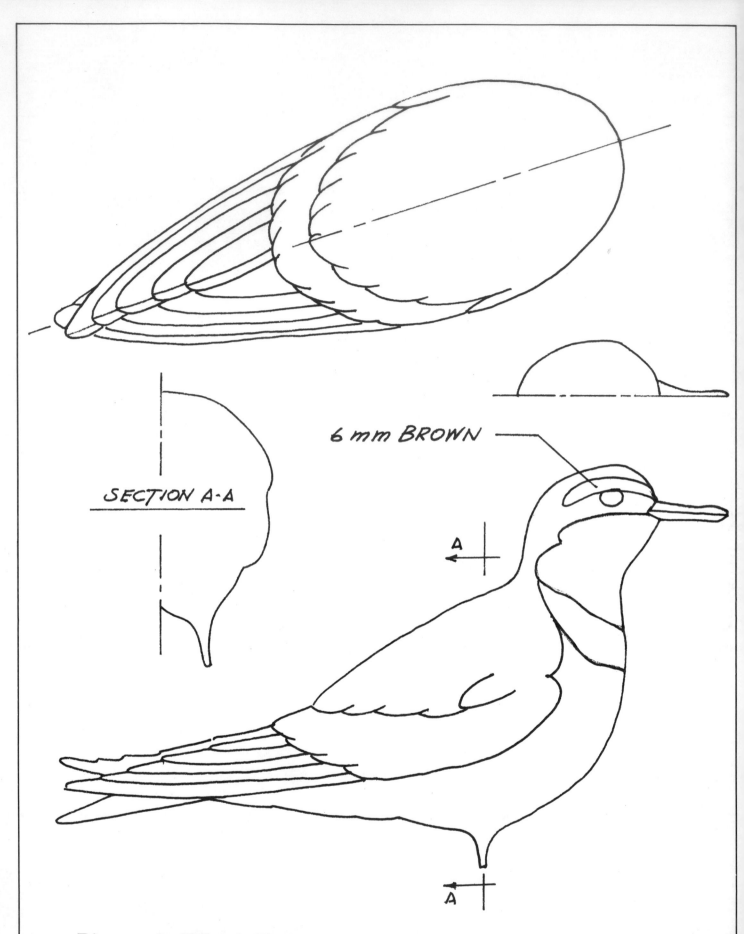

SECTION A-A

6 mm BROWN

A

A

Diagram 1. Wilson's Plover.

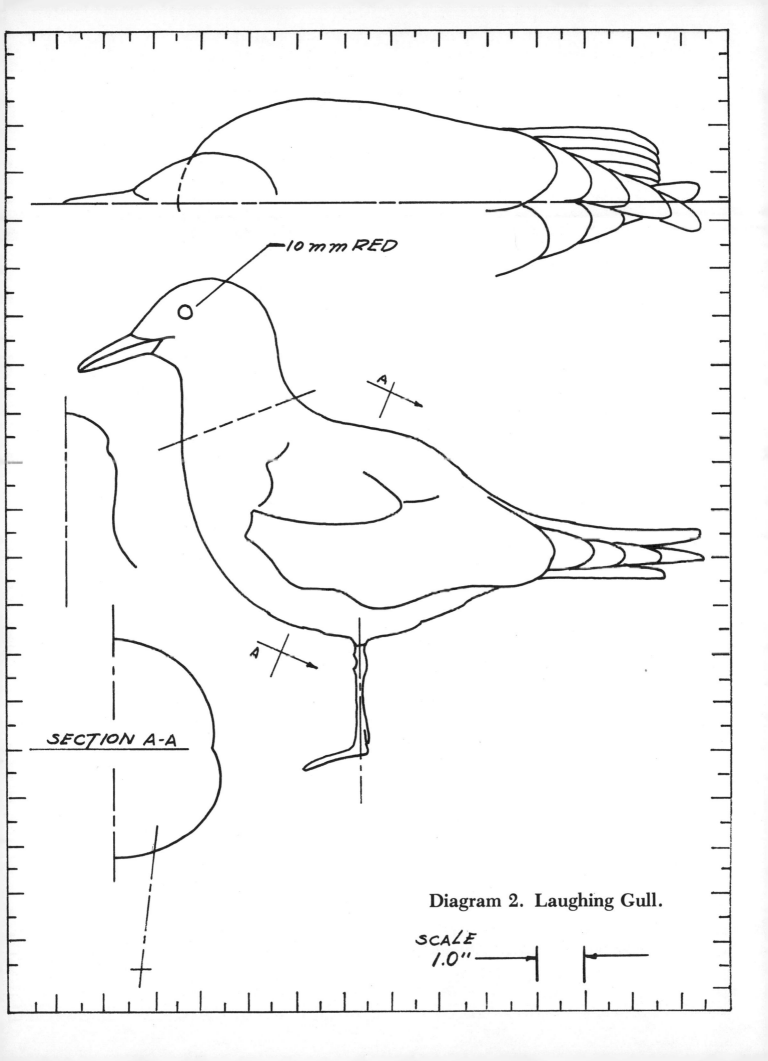

10 m m RED

SECTION A-A

Diagram 2. Laughing Gull.

SCALE
1.0"

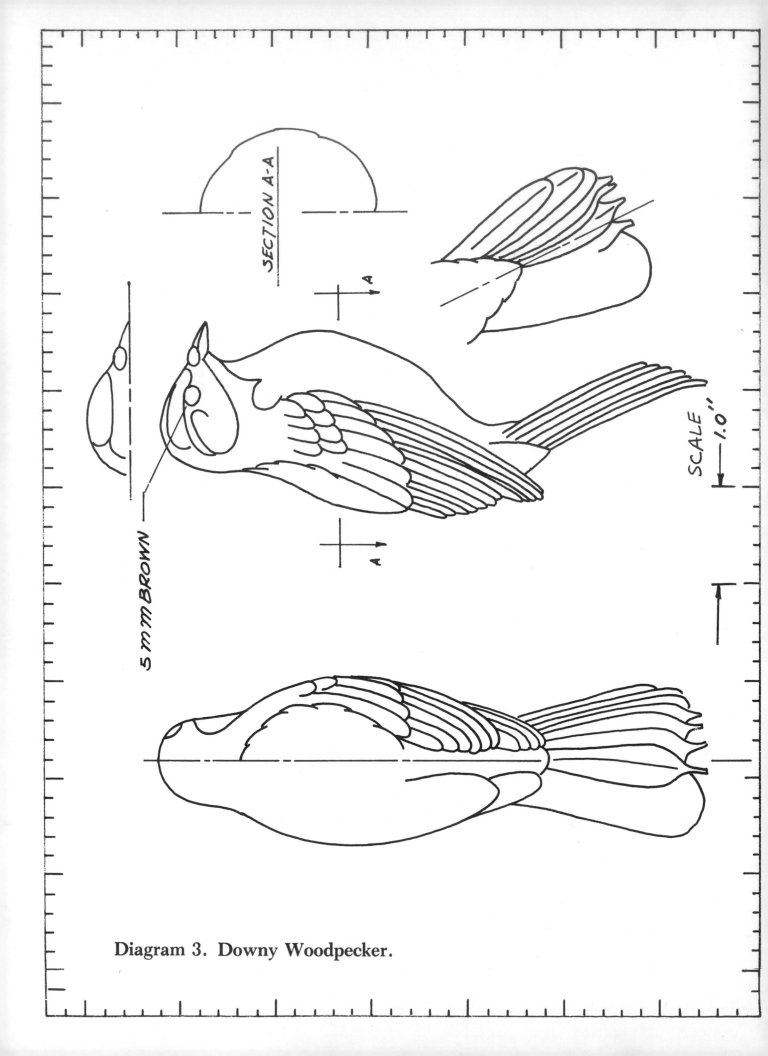

SECTION A-A

A

A

5 mm BROWN

SCALE 1.0"

Diagram 3. Downy Woodpecker.

II. Woodpeckers

Structurally very similar to perching birds, with which they are often grouped, woodpeckers are readily distinguished by their strong, sharply pointed bills that are ideally suited for chopping and digging into tree trunks and branches for wood-boring insects. All except the three-toed variety have two toes in front and two in the back. The arrangement of their toes and their stiff tails, which are used as props, enable woodpeckers to sit upright against a tree while pecking a nest hole or searching for food. When they abandon their nests, other birds often use them. Woodpeckers are one of the few groups of birds that store food.

Downy Woodpecker

Of the twenty-three varieties of woodpeckers that inhabit North America, the Downy Woodpecker (*Dendrocopos pubescens*) is the smallest, measuring just under six inches in length. The Downy is often confused with its larger cousin, the Hairy Woodpecker (*Dendrocopos villosus*). The reason for this confusion is that not only do both varieties have essentially the same range—most

Figure 15.   The Downy Woodpecker.

Figure 14.   *Three pieces of wood may be used to carve either the Downy or the Hairy Woodpecker.*

of the United States and the forested parts of Canada—but also both are almost the same in appearance: black and white wings and heads, white backs, and red patches on the back of the heads of the males. Only the Downy, however, has dark bars on its white outer tail feathers. Because they are so similar, the Downy carving pattern (see Diagram 3) can, with a simple adjustment, also be used to carve a replica of a Hairy Woodpecker. To adjust the pattern for the Hairy Woodpecker, connect the hash marks at the margins of the Downy pattern with straight lines. Then redraw the pattern by the squares method on a separate piece of paper with four vertical and four horizontal lines to the inch. (This paper is sometimes called quad paper.) In addition lengthen the bill on the redrawn pattern by approximately one-fourth inch. A six-millimeter

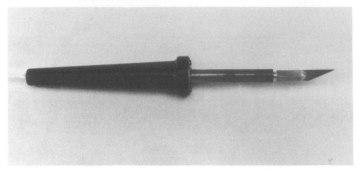

Figure 16.   A hot knife.

brown eye should be substituted for the one indicated on the Downy pattern.

For either the Downy or Hairy Woodpecker carving, three pieces of stock may be used with the lines of grain running parallel to the tail, wings, and bill respectively (see Figure 14). Rather than assemble all three blocks at the outset, you may find it easier first to shape the head, body, and wings generally as a unit prior to incorporating the tail block. This method affords your knife better access to the underside of the wings than will be possible once the tail block has been incorporated.

With carving and shaping completed, use a pyroelectric pen to burn in tail feather barbs on both sides and some feather details on the breast and head. Then paint the entire carving with white gesso. Next, paint all black, white, and red areas

Figure 17.   With carving completed, the Downy Woodpecker is now ready for feather detailing with a pyroelectric pen.

Figure 18.   The Downy Woodpecker on its base.

(assuming a male) with acrylic paint, allowing a bit more black to invade white areas than may be indicated by pictures you have accumulated as reference material. With a hot knife (see Figure 16), available at most hobby shops, burn in the remaining feather details in the white areas and partially into the black areas. The temperature of the hot knife tends to remove the black acrylic paint, thereby allowing the white gesso underneath to show. Thus the solid line separating black and white will now become feathered as if one shade has been blended into the other. White wing markings can also be produced in this manner. You should take note, however, that too much burning, or holding the hot knife in one spot too long, can cause a burned wood tone. Should this happen, repeat the process with the gesso, acrylic paint, and hot knife. You can usually repeat this process one or two times before paint buildup becomes a problem.

Red-Headed Woodpecker

Other woodpeckers may sport a red cap, but the Red-headed Woodpecker (*Melanerpes erythrocephalus*) is unmistakable with its scarlet coloration from the collar up. White rump and wing patches and a black back comprise the remainder of the adult plumage. The bird does not spend its entire life so vividly adorned, however: as if nature intended the period of apprenticeship to be marked by lack of pigmentation, juveniles are ash brown, which caused some early naturalists to believe the young were a different species.

The Red-head's diet primarily consists of fruit and insects in the summer and stored acorns in the winter. The bird also consumes a large num-

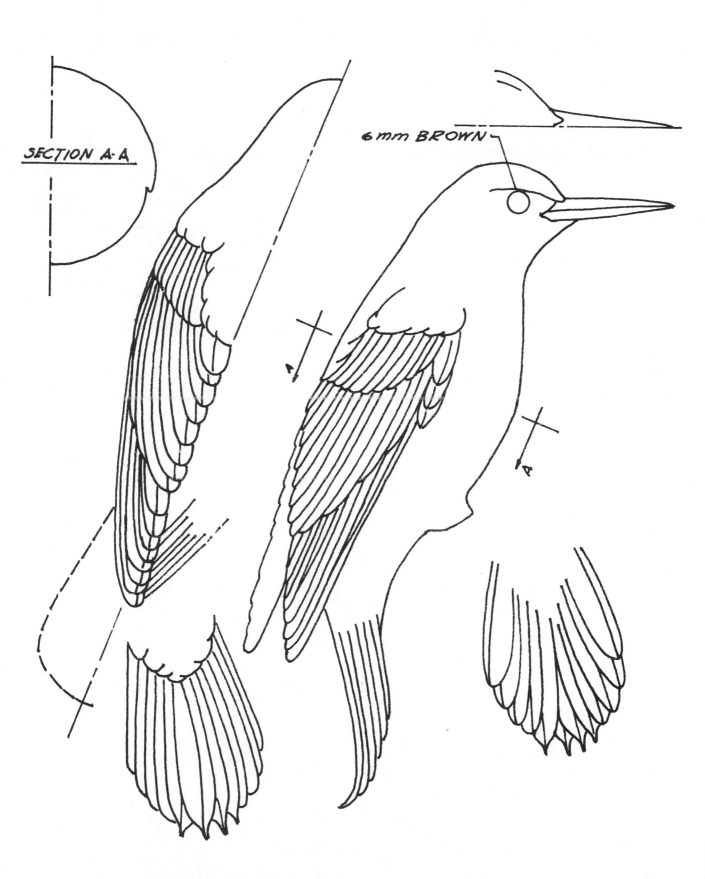

SECTION A·A

6mm BROWN

Diagram 4. Red-headed Woodpecker.

Figure 19. Underside of the Red-headed Woodpecker.

ber of grasshoppers that it prepares at "butcher block" stumps by first ripping off legs and wing covers and then eating the rest. Like all members of the woodpecker clan, the Red-headed Woodpecker's consumption of harmful grubs and beetles makes it a desirable as well as an attractive bird to have about.

The carving pictured here was made from three blocks of wood—for head, body, and tail respectively—glued together. An alternate technique is to make the head and body from one block of wood, with the grain running parallel to the wings; the beak is then carved from a five-sixteenths-inch wood dowel inserted appropriately into the head. For the tail, carve a slot between the upper and lower coverts and insert preshaped feathers either individually or in pairs. Before you insert the middle four feathers, hold them with needle-nose pliers in the path of the steam

Figure 21.   Front view of the Red-headed Woodpecker.

from a tea kettle while bending and shaping the trailing margins in a typical woodpecker "tail prop" configuration.

The feet may be constructed from piano wire (also called *music wire*), using the procedure outlined in Diagram 16, but this procedure must be modified to create the Red-headed Woodpecker's two forward and two rear toes.

Figure 20.   The Red-headed Woodpecker on its base.

III. Perching Birds

Perching or Passerine Birds comprise over fifty percent of the world's bird population. All the birds in this group are medium to small in size. They also are all land birds with four toes, all on the same level and never webbed, on each foot. The hind toes are as long as the middle front toe; this arrangement contributes to the birds' perching ability. All perching birds have twelve tail feathers.

Black-Capped Chickadee

There are seven chickadee species in North America. All derive their surname from their call of chick-a-dee-dee, which may vary among the different species in tonal quality, range, and rapidity. Except to the most discriminating eye, all species are similar in pattern, size, and disposition. The Black-capped Chickadee has the largest range, but it is perhaps better known in the northeast, where it is the state bird of Maine and Massachusetts. While the Black-capped Chickadee was the basis for the pattern and depicted carving, the pattern can be used to carve any of the remaining chickadee species with little or no modification. Table 1 provides nominal lengths and basic color information for all chickadee species.

An option is to carve the bird's abdomen and flanks a bit stouter than shown in Figure 26. This will give the bird the appearance of attempting to insulate itself from the cold, and for the carver, a stouter bird requires less backcutting on the underside of the wings. Should you mount your carving as shown in the photographs, only the toes are exposed to view, thereby eliminating the need for making feet. If you want to make feet, however, the method described in Diagram 16, but without the foot thread winding, is best suited for the various chickadee species.

Eastern Bluebird

The bluebird is well known in American folklore. The settlers of Plymouth colony called it the "Blue Robin." Its spring arrival in the north was once equated with the day the sap started up the trunk of the sugar maple. In more recent times the bluebird has been the subject for songs of happiness and hope. Although it is a member of the thrush family, which is found the world over, the bluebird belongs to a subdivision that originated and remains in North America.

The depicted carving is of the Eastern Bluebird (*Sialia sialis*), the state bird of Missouri and New York. The pattern can also be used to carve the Western Bluebird (*Sialia mexicana*) and the Mountain Bluebird (*Sialia currucoides*), the state bird of Idaho and Nevada. For carving purposes these three species are generally the same size and shape. The main difference among the species is coloration.

Male Eastern Bluebirds have bright blue wings and backs, a chestnut throat and breast, and a white belly and undertail. Female coloration is similar to that of the male but duller and grayer on top, with most of the blue tones in the wings and tail. The female normally incubates four to six pale blue eggs (.84 × .62 inches in size) for about twelve days. Since they are speckle-breasted and grayish, young bluebirds look more thrush-like than do adults. The young have no red but always some hint of blue in their wings and tail.

The Eastern Bluebird, formerly seen in great numbers in cities and towns, now prefers the abundant trees and vegetation of the open country-side. The Eastern Bluebird population has been drastically reduced over the past fifty years or so, with only slight increases from time to time. Among the reasons for this bird's decline is the shortage of nesting sites and the severe competition for these sites from more aggressive birds such as Red-winged Blackbirds and House Sparrows.

The hardier Western Bluebird has the same colors as its eastern relatives but they are arranged differently. The male's throat is blue and the chestnut color on his breast extends to the shoulders and back.

The Mountain Bluebird has no red coloration. Except for an off-white belly, the male is a vivid turquoise blue during the breeding season. At

Figure 22.   Front view of the Black-capped Chickadee. Note the angle of the head, which makes it appear that the bird is viewing us.

Figure 25.   Top view of the Black-capped Chickadee.

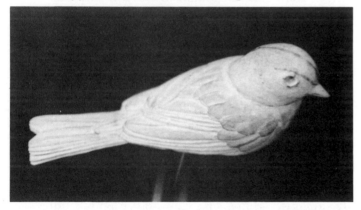

Figure 23.   Black-capped Chickadee seen from the side before painting.

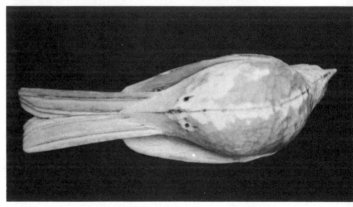

Figure 26.   Underside of the Black-capped Chickadee carving.

Figure 24.   A painted Black-capped Chickadee.

Figure 27.   The completed Black-capped Chickadee carving.

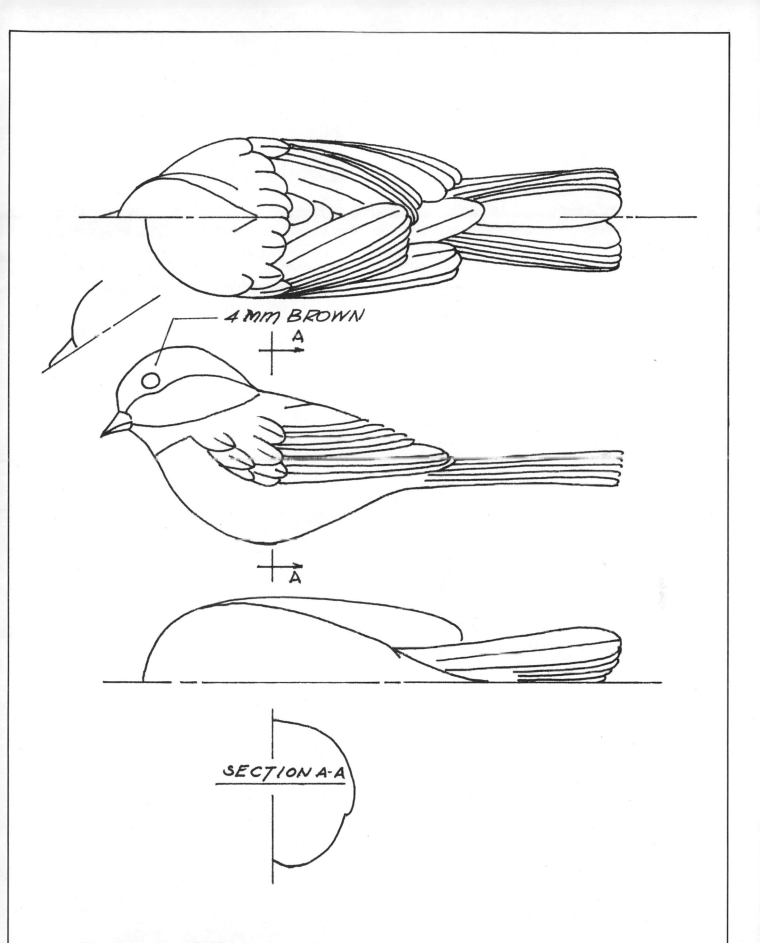

4 MM BROWN

A

A

SECTION A-A

Diagram 5. Black-capped Chickadee.

Figure 28.   The Eastern Bluebird.

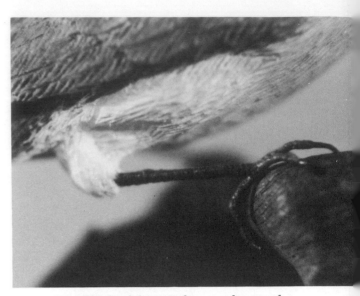

Figure 31.   *Bluebird foot made according to the procedure outlined in Diagram 16.*

Figure 29.   *The head of the Bluebird is rotated about forty-five degrees with respect to the body.*

Figure 32.   *Bluebird looking away from the camera. The wing on the near side is undercut.*

Figure 30.   *Close-up of the head of the Eastern Bluebird carving.*

Figure 33.   *Bluebird carving mounted on its stand. The wing on the near side, which is not undercut, almost disappears into the breast.*

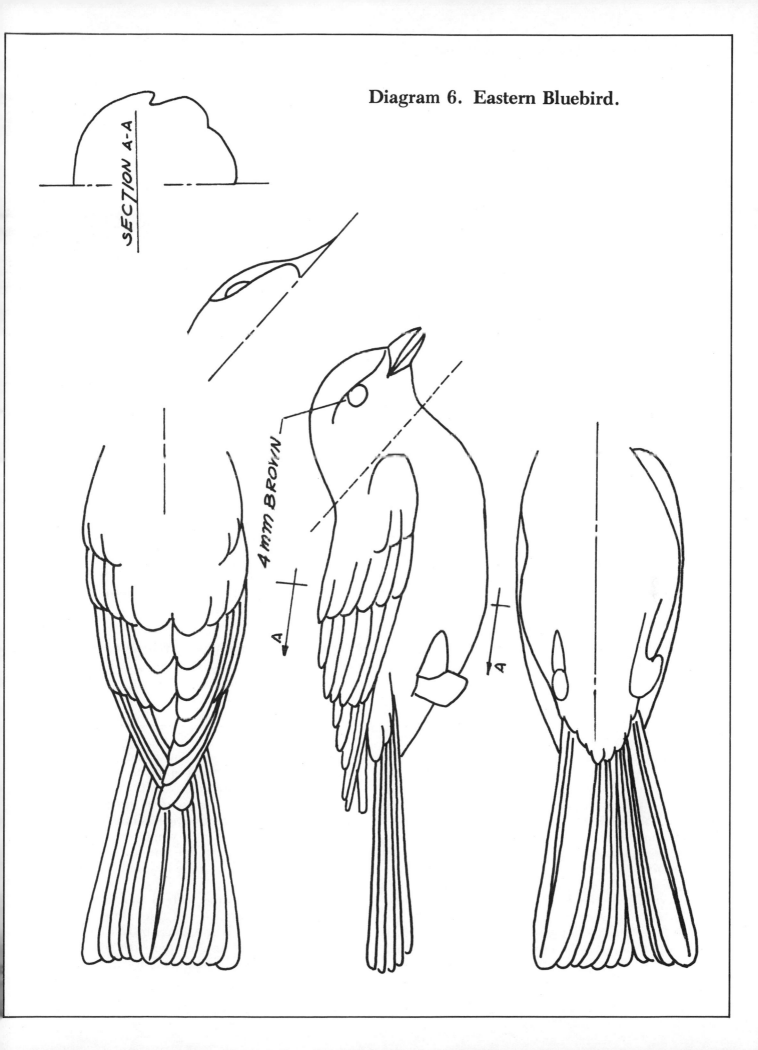

Diagram 6. Eastern Bluebird.

TABLE 1.   General Information on Chickadees

Species	Length (inches)	Coloration	Range	Additional Notes
Black-capped (*Parus atricapillus*)	4.75 to 5.75	Black cap and bib, white cheeks and breast, gray back, buff sides, wing feathers gray edged with white	Northern states and Canada	Rustier sides and shinier cheeks than Carolina, whose range it may invade
Carolina (*Parus carolinensis*)	4.25 to 4.75	Black cap and bib with sharp separation between black bib and white breast; white cheeks, gray back, buff sides; wing feathers are gray with light gray edges	Southern states	Smaller bib and shorter tail than Black-capped
Mountain (*Parus gambeli*)	5.00 to 5.75	Black cap with white line above each eye, black bib, white cheeks and breast	Mountainous areas from southwest Texas west to California and north to British Columbia and Alberta	Only chickadee with a white eye stripe
Mexican (*Parus sclateri*)	4.75 to 6.50	Black cap and large black throat patch, gray sides	Southern Arizona and northern Mexico	Only chickadee in its limited range
Gray-headed (*Parus cinctus*)	4.75 to 5.50	Dark gray cap, black bib, white cheeks, dusky sides and back	Edge of Alaskan and west Canadian tundra	. . .
Boreal (*Parus hudsonicus*)	5.00 to 5.50	Dark brown cap, buffy brown flanks, black bib	From northern states to the freeze line of Canada and Alaska	Only chickadee with a brown cap
Chestnut-backed (*Parus rufescens*)	4.50 to 5.00	Chestnut back and sides, white cheeks, sooty cap, black bib	Pacific coast from southern Alaska to southern California and inland to Montana	Has no whistled song; calls are hoarse

other times of the year, particularly fall and winter, his plumage has tints of dull brown—the predominant color of the female throughout the year.

The pattern for the bluebird carving is shown in Diagram 6. The carving requires two blocks of wood: one for the head, the other for the body, wings, and tail, with the grain running parallel to the beak and tail.

You will note in the pictures of the finished carving that the head has been rotated about forty-five degrees with respect to the body (see Figure 29). The degree of head rotation for your carving depends largely on the stand on which you will mount the completed carving. The stand and carving should be coordinated (see Figure 33). In addition, the wing opposite to the direction in which the bird is looking is undercut (see Figure 32), whereas the wing on the bill side is carved so that it almost disappears into the breast. Undercutting only a single wing serves to orient the body and wings with the turned head. Should you choose not to rotate the head, undercut both wings.

A deviation from the pattern was to flare the tail feathers slightly on one side while stacking them on the other. While it may be true that birds do not necessarily arrange their tail feathers in a nice neat package when perching, this fact had nothing to do with the deviation from the tail pattern. Rather the deviation was necessary because of an inappropriately positioned knot being discovered when I was well into the carving process.

When the carving is completed, barbs and other feather details can be produced with pyro-electric pen and chip-carving knife.

Red-Winged Blackbird

For even the novice bird-watcher, one glimpse of flashing red epaulets against a solid black background is all that is required to identify a male Red-winged Blackbird (*Agelaius phoeniceus*). Field recognition of the female is quite a different matter, however, for she is drab brown with streaked underparts. A bird-watcher may wonder to what species the female belongs when she is seen without her mate. Colored as she is, the female becomes quite obscure as she blends in with her surroundings.

The Red-winged Blackbird sometimes builds its nest in trees but most often builds it on the ground in waterside brush. The nest is a basket of rushes filled with peat and chunks of rotten wood lined with soft, fine grasses. The three to five eggs are bluish-green spotted with brown and purple. Naked and blind when born, young Red-winged Blackbirds are usually able to leave the nest in about ten days, becoming proficient swimmers and climbers before they can fly. The male does not share directly in nest activities, but instead guards the breeding territory by boldly attacking any and all that come near. When the nesting season is over, the birds become inconspicuous while they shed all their tail feathers at once and new ones grow in. Unlike other birds that molt and replace their tail feathers a pair at a time, the Red-winged Blackbird seems to be able to get along for a time during the fall of the year without the steering and balancing mechanism the tail feathers provide. When the new full-

Figure 35. The Red-winged Blackbird on its stand.

Figure 34. Since the right wing (on far side of bird) of the Red-winged Blackbird protrudes slightly upward, the grain of the body block should be parallel to the wing.

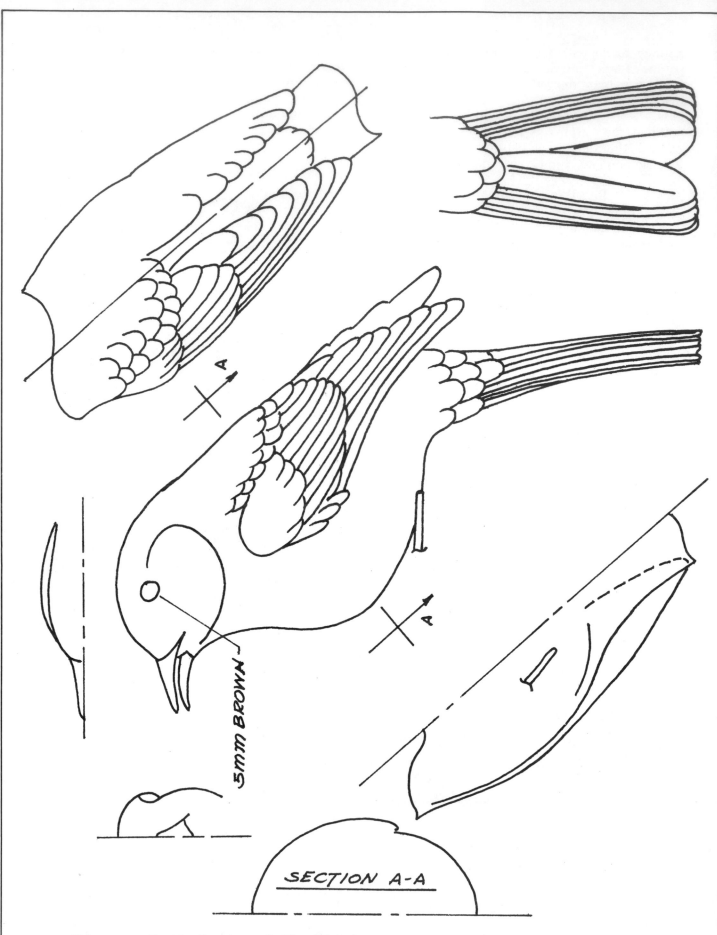

5mm BROWN

SECTION A-A

Diagram 7. Red-winged Blackbird.

Figure 36. *Close-up of the head of a Red-winged Blackbird carving.*

Figure 37. *Completed Red-winged Blackbird carving seen from above.*

length tails are in place, the birds swarm to community roosts.

Make the head, body, and tail from three pieces of wood as was done with the Downy Woodpecker carving (see Figure 14). As you can see from the pattern, the attitude of the bird causes the right wing to protrude slightly upward, which makes that wing especially subject to accidental breakage. In order to provide better strength in this area, the line of the grain for the body block should be parallel to the protruding wing.

Totally black carved birds are probably the most difficult to paint. Black, especially when applied directly from the tube, can produce an extremely flat appearance, void of body or substance. To correct this problem, carve at least a few, if not all, individual feathers on the back, rump, and flanks in addition to those usually carved on the wings and tail. Adding cobalt blue and burnt umber to the black paint will also help. When the painting is complete, score the head and the tips of the feathers with a hot knife and then apply a spray matte finish for sheen.

Yellow-Headed Blackbird

Noisy and conspicuous are two words that aptly describe the Yellow-headed Blackbird. Its song is a piercing string of notes that is often compared to the sound produced by a swinging rusty gate hinge, and it is sung with seemingly painful twists and turns, as if to demonstrate the bird's inability to accept what it hears. What the Yellow-

headed Blackbird lacks in melody, however, is more than compensated for by its coloration. As the scientific name *Xanthocephalus xanthocephalus* (*xanthus*, yellow; *cephalus*, head) partly implies, the head and upper breast of the male are bright yellow. This vivid coloration plus white wing patches provide a striking contrast to the remainder of the bird's plumage, which is typical of other Blackbirds.

Though not as colorfully adorned as her mate, the hard-working female is no less beautiful. A brownish bird with soft yellow hues limited to her face, throat, and breast, she builds the nests, which are woven open cups secured to cattails and reeds. Nesting sites include prairies, fresh water marshes, and borders of lakes in the western plains of the United States and throughout California. The species' large feet and strong toes enable these birds to walk on mud and floating vegetation common to the nesting areas. The three or four eggs (1.00 × .70 inches in size) that the female incubates are gray-green and heavily speckled with brown or gray. The birds breed in large colonies that can range into the thousands and feed mostly on insects, resorting to grain when it is available.

In the pattern the bird's upper chest is especially large (see Diagram 8). You may note from photographs of this bird taken in the wild that the bird's chest frequently appears to be rather large in proportion to the rest of its body. The Yellow-headed Blackbird, like many other species, often separates feathers in this region as a means of insulating its body, to attract members of the opposite sex, or simply because it is riled. Whether

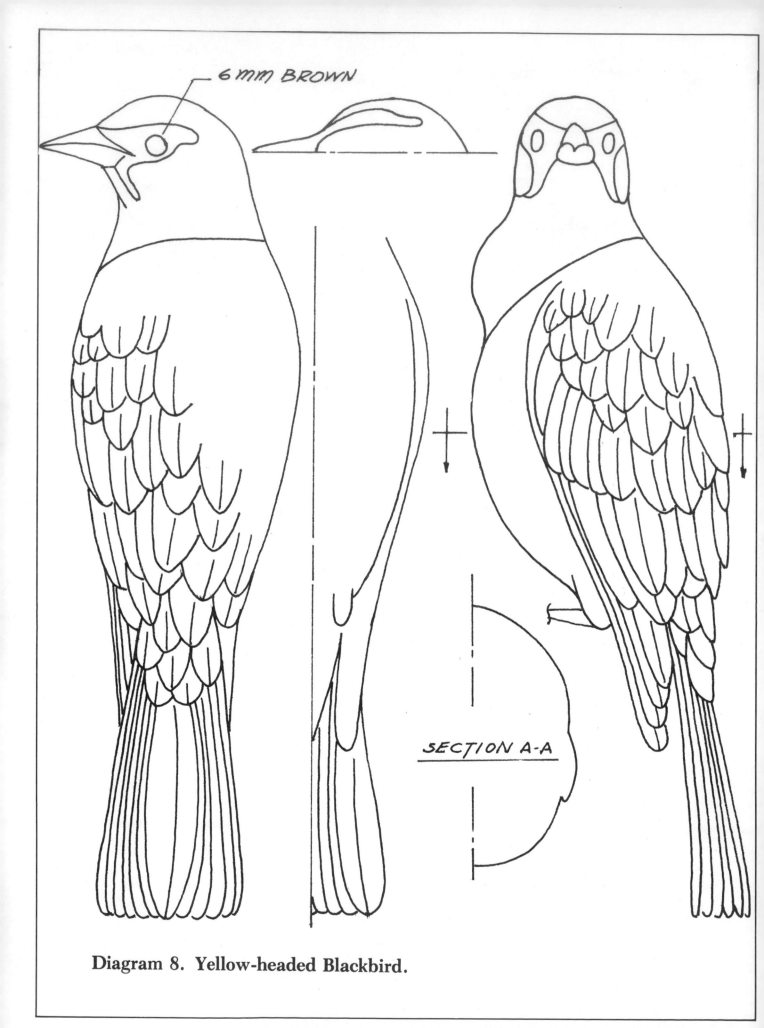

6 MM BROWN

SECTION A-A

Diagram 8. Yellow-headed Blackbird.

Figure 38.   The Yellow-headed Blackbird.

Figure 40.   Side view showing the large chest of the Yellow-headed Blackbird.

Figure 39.   Front view of the Yellow-headed Blackbird.

Figure 41.   Yellow-headed Blackbird looking over its shoulder. Note the feather detailing incised with a pyroelectric pen and chip-carving knife.

Figure 42.   Head of a Yellow-headed Blackbird.

Figure 43.   Feet of a Yellow-headed Blackbird. For construction see Diagram 16.

or not to include such an enlarged chest as indicated in the pattern is left to the discretion of the carver.

The chest of the depicted carving was made from the body block. The grain of this block is parallel to the bird's wings and tail and, therefore, runs across the lines of the chest feathers. As a result, the chest area of this carving is compacted since these feathers could not be undercut without breaking and splitting away. I suggest that the chest area of your carving be made from a separate piece of stock with the line of the grain running at an angle of approximately thirty degrees to the grain of the body block. This angle should allow the feathers to be better structured and more separated.

Lichtenstein's Oriole

Orioles are among the most colorful of the North American birds. The males are boldly patterned in black and yellow, orange, or chestnut, while the females are mostly olive and yellow with little pattern.

Figures 44 through 47 depict the carving of a Lichtenstein's Oriole made from the pattern on Diagram 9. This oriole is perhaps best known to the residents of the Rio Grande Valley of Texas where it makes its home much of the year. The bird's head was carved at an oblique angle to give the impression that the bird is looking with its left eye at some object on the ground. This orientation of the head is an optional deviation from the pattern. Should you not be familiar with this oriole or wish to carve another member of the oriole family, Table 2 provides each species' dimensions so that you can change the pattern appropriately.

Note that Table 2 lists the orioles that were until recently the eight identified species, but two of the species, the Baltimore and Bullock's Orioles, have been grouped together for taxo-

Figure 44.   Lichtenstein's Oriole.

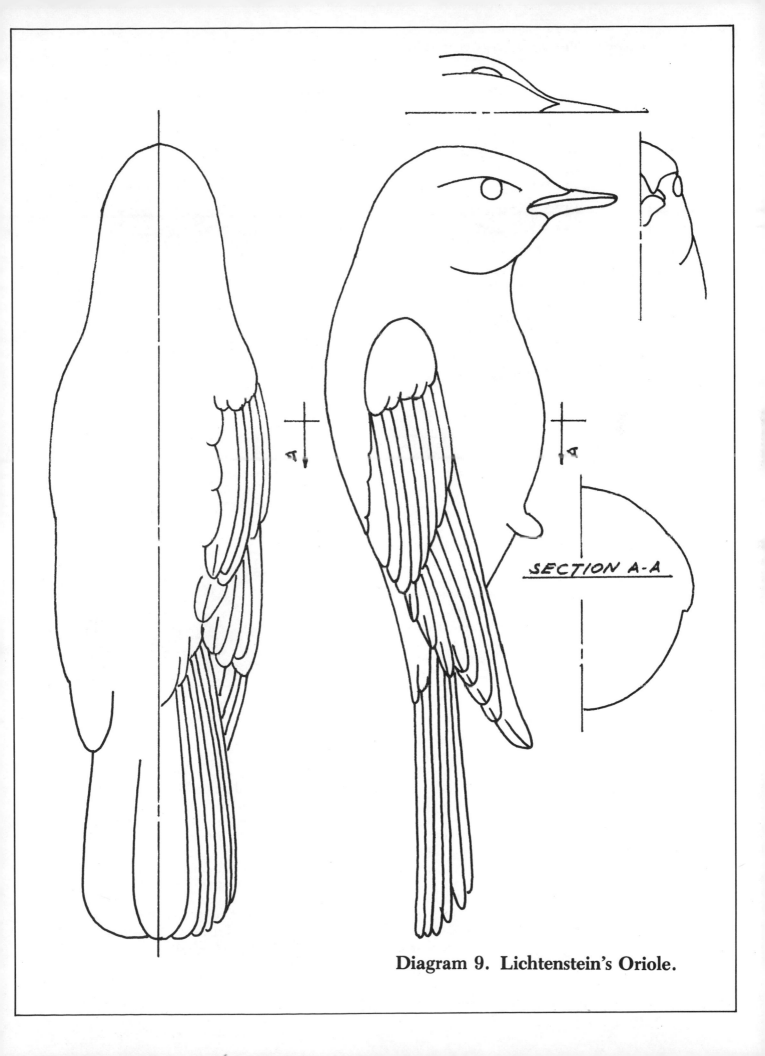

SECTION A-A

Diagram 9. Lichtenstein's Oriole.

Figure 46.   Close-up of the head of Lichtenstein's Oriole.

Figure 45.   *Lichtenstein's Oriole looking at the ground with its left eye.*

Figure 47.   *Another view of Lichtenstein's Oriole. Once again note the optional turned head.*

nomical purposes as the Northern Oriole since in areas where both the Baltimore and Bullock's Orioles are found, hybridization may take place. (As a matter of definition, a species is a group of organisms that for biological—not geographical or other—reasons cannot breed outside its group.) It is doubtful that residents of Maryland would agree with the taxonomists' recent judgment since long ago they made the Baltimore Oriole their state bird. Nevertheless, the Bullock's Oriole does resemble the Baltimore, both being dressed in Lord Baltimore's colors of orange and black, with the primary difference between the two groups of birds being color arrangement.

Brown Thrasher

As one might correctly assume from the long bill, the Brown Thrasher (*Toxostoma rufum*) is primarily a ground-feeding bird, with beetles, caterpillars, and other insects making up the bulk of its diet. Some people believe the bird gets its name from the way it thrashes among fallen leaves in search of insects. Others think the name is simply derived from the way it thrashes its long tail. The Brown Thrasher is found in eastern North America and is the state bird of Georgia.

The long tail, slender bill, and short wings identify the Brown Thrasher as a member of the same family (Mimidae) as the Mockingbird and the Catbird. Less of a mimic than the Mockingbird, the Thrasher is a much better singer than the Catbird. A singing pose has been suggested by the pattern in Diagram 10. Proceed with carving in much the same way as for the other projects described thus far. The Brown Thrasher's coloration includes a reddish-brown head and back, white wing bars, and whitish underparts with dark streaks.

TABLE 2.   General Information on Orioles

Species	Length (inches)	Coloration	Range	Additional Notes
Baltimore (*Icterus galbula*)	6.5	Male: orange breast, rump, and tail corners; black head, wings, and tail; white-edged wing feathers Female and young: orange-olive upper parts, yellow-orange under parts, white wing bars	Central Alberta east to Nova Scotia and south to Texas and Georgia. Winters in Central America	Hybridizes with Bullock's Oriole (see below)
Bullock's (*Icterus bullockii*)	7.0	Male: black crown, eye stripes, back, and tail; white wing patches; orange cheeks, underparts, rump, and base of tail Female and young: olive-gray head and back, yellow breast, white belly and wing bars	British Columbia east to Saskatchewan and south to central Mexico. Winters in Central America	Combined taxonomically with the Baltimore Oriole as the Northern Oriole (*Icterus galbula bullockii*)
Hooded (*Icterus cucullatus*)	7.0	Male: orange hood, belly, and rump; black throat, wings, and tail; wing feathers edged with white Female and young: olive head and back, yellow belly, white wingbars	Central California to southern Mexico. Winters in Mexico	Hybridizes with Bullock's Oriole
Lichtenstein's (*Icterus guloris*)	8.5	Male: same as Hooded Oriole except it has broad yellow-orange upper wing patch Female and young: dark grayish-brown wings and yellow-olive back	Southern Texas and Mexico	Distinguished from Hooded Oriole by larger size, heavier bill, and upper wing patch
Black-headed (*Icterus graduacauda*)	8.0	Male: black head, wings, and tail; chestnut rump and underparts; wing feathers edged with white Female and young: same as male except back is olive green	Southern Manitoba east to Massachusetts and south to central Mexico and Florida. Winters in Mexico and South America	· · ·
Orchard (*Icterus spurius*)	6.0	Male: black head, wings, and tail; chestnut rump and underparts; wing feathers edged with white Female and young: olive head and back, yellow underparts, white wing bars	Southern Manitoba east to Massachusetts and south to central Mexico and Florida. Winters in Mexico and South America	· · ·
Spotted-breasted (*Icterus pectoralis*)	7.5	Male and female: orange crown and underparts; black throat, wings, and back; black spots at sides of breast; white wing patches. Young: no breast spots	Southern Florida and from southern Mexico to Costa Rica	Introduced to Florida
Scott's (*Icterus parisorum*)	7.0	Male: black head, breast, back, wings, and tail; lemon-yellow belly and rump; wings edged with white Female and young: molted olive back, yellow underparts, white wing bars	Southeastern California to West Texas and south to northern Mexico	· · ·

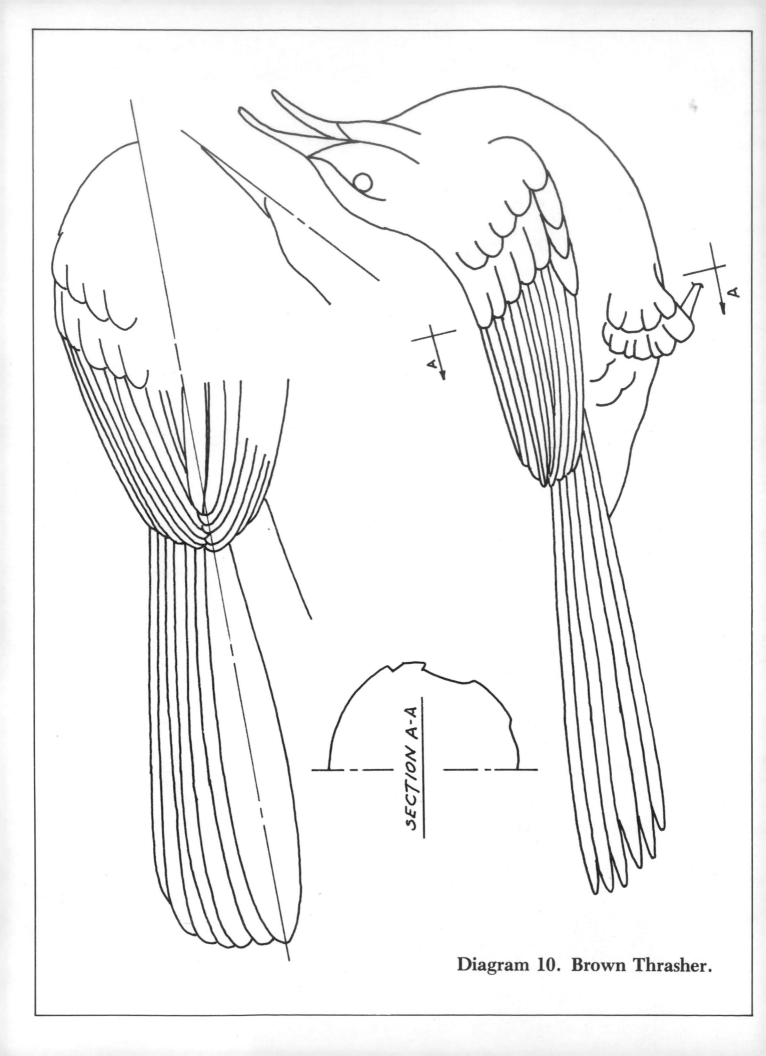

Diagram 10. Brown Thrasher.

SECTION A-A

Figure 48.   *The Brown Thrasher.*

Figure 51.   Close-up of the Brown Thrasher's head and long bill.

Figure 49.   The tail of the Brown Thrasher seen from an angle.

Figure 52.   Another view of the Brown Thrasher.

Figure 50.   Front view of the Brown Thrasher showing the long tail.

Figure 53.   Underside of Brown Thrasher's tail.

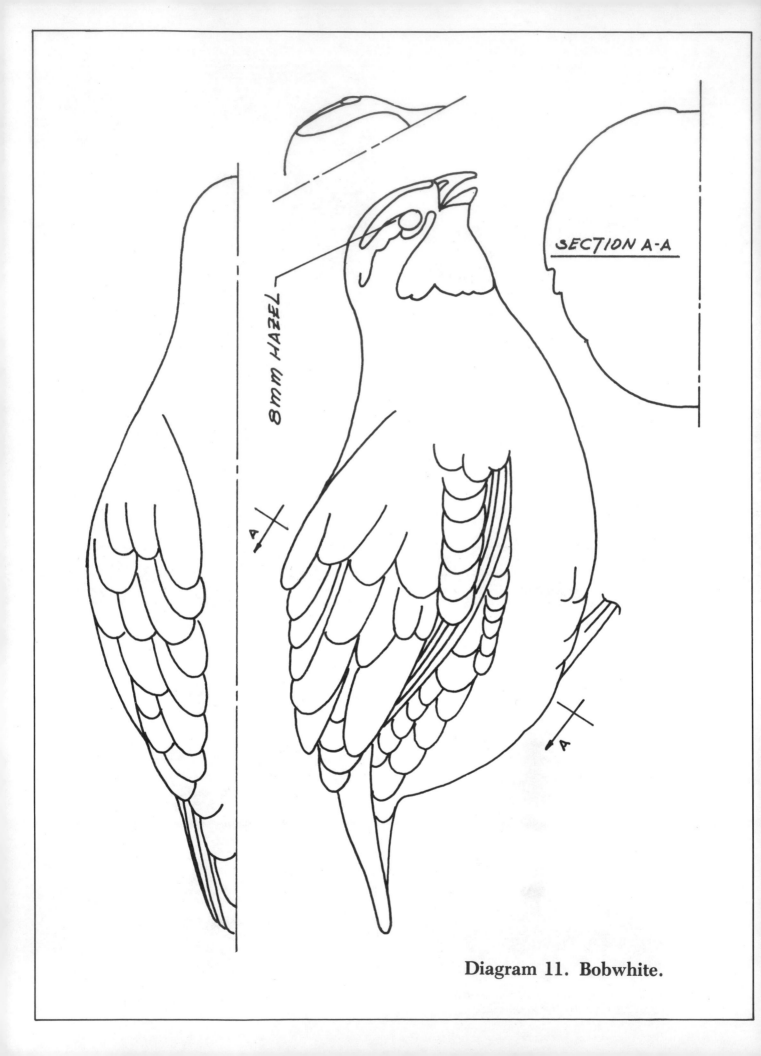

8mm HAZEL

SECTION A-A

Diagram 11. Bobwhite.

IV. Gallinaceous Birds

Gallinaceous, or fowl-like, Birds are land birds with heavy bodies; chickens belong to this order. All Gallinaceous Birds are scratchers, having well-developed feet and toes for foraging in the ground for seeds and insects. When flushed, the birds burst into flight very fast, often from a sitting position, but usually they do not fly very far.

Since Gallinaceous Birds, especially the males, are so intricately colored, creating their likenesses is usually more of a challenge to your painting ability than to your carving ability. Color photographs are helpful to the carver for duplicating plumage coloration. In order to produce an accurate replica, try to get an actual skin for first-hand observation. Museums and wildlife refuges are excellent sources for stuffed specimens. Since Gallinaceous Birds are usually game birds, friends who hunt can also be a source for fresh kills. The simplest way to preserve a fresh kill is to place it in the freezer, removing it only as necessary for reference. Unfortunately this is only a temporary method, since body shrinkage and feather discoloration will become noticeable with time.

Figure 54. The Bobwhite.

Figure 55. Side view of the completed Bobwhite carving.

Bobwhite

"American Partridge," "Quail," and simply "Bird" are but a few of the colloquial names that continue to be used to identify this upland game bird (*Colinus virginianus*). Of the several names, however, it seems the bird itself prefers *Bobwhite*, for it is most persistent in proclaiming this choice, especially during the mating season. Once a staple food for colonial America and long a much-sought prize for leisure-time hunters, the Bobwhite is to many simply a songbird with an unmistakable, familiar, whistling call. Whether the specimens are pinkish brown, as they are in the Northeast, or a combination of reds and blacks, as in the South and Mexico, the tune remains the same.

Bobwhites usually nest on the ground in a hollow that has been scratched out by the male and then filled by him with grasses and weeds. Some nests may have arched roofs of grass to help conceal the white eggs, which may number up to fifteen.

Once hatched, the brood is able to leave the nest almost immediately. Wings develop rapidly;

a young bird is able to fly short distances in about three weeks.

The depicted carving was made from two pieces of white pine, each with the line of the grain running parallel to the beak; the two pieces were glued together at the center line. A third piece of stock was inserted into the body for the tail. An alternate approach is to have the grain of the body block run parallel to the tail, and to use a separate piece of stock with its grain running parallel to the beak for the head. This alternate procedure allows the head to be oriented to a position other than looking straight ahead. More importantly this procedure provides a better grain orientation for undercutting the body and wing feathers. Should you wish to undercut these feathers, first carve all the feathers on the outer side, which will tell you whether all the feathers lie properly and enable you to correct the position

of any that do not. Once the underside of a feather has been cut, there usually is not enough stock left to make any modifications. Undercut the feathers with a knife. Half a hacksaw blade with about twenty teeth to the inch works especially well (see Figure 57). Use the procedure outlined in Diagram 18 for making the feet.

Possibly the most difficult part of the Bobwhite project is painting it once the carving is completed. The coloration of this game bird is complex and, as previously stated, may vary with location. As a result you may wish to do nothing more than apply some stain and varnish, which, in addition to providing a protective coating, will also accentuate the details of the carving. Should you wish to tackle the painting, you will need to obtain several photographs of either a male or female bird and, if possible, a stuffed bird or fresh kill.

Figure 56.   Bobwhite breast and belly feathers carved individually.

Figure 58.   Bobwhite tail made from separate piece of stock and inserted into the body block.

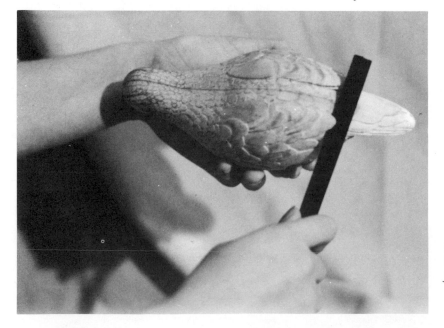

Figure 57.   Hacksaw blades broken in half work well for backcutting feathers.

Figure 59. *Front view of the Bobwhite.*

Figure 62. *Rear view of the Bobwhite.*

Figure 60. *A fresh-killed Bobwhite: almost a necessity to carve and paint a Bobwhite accurately.*

Figure 63. *Close-up of the Bobwhite head.*

Figure 61. *Right foot and toes of the Bobwhite (actual size).*

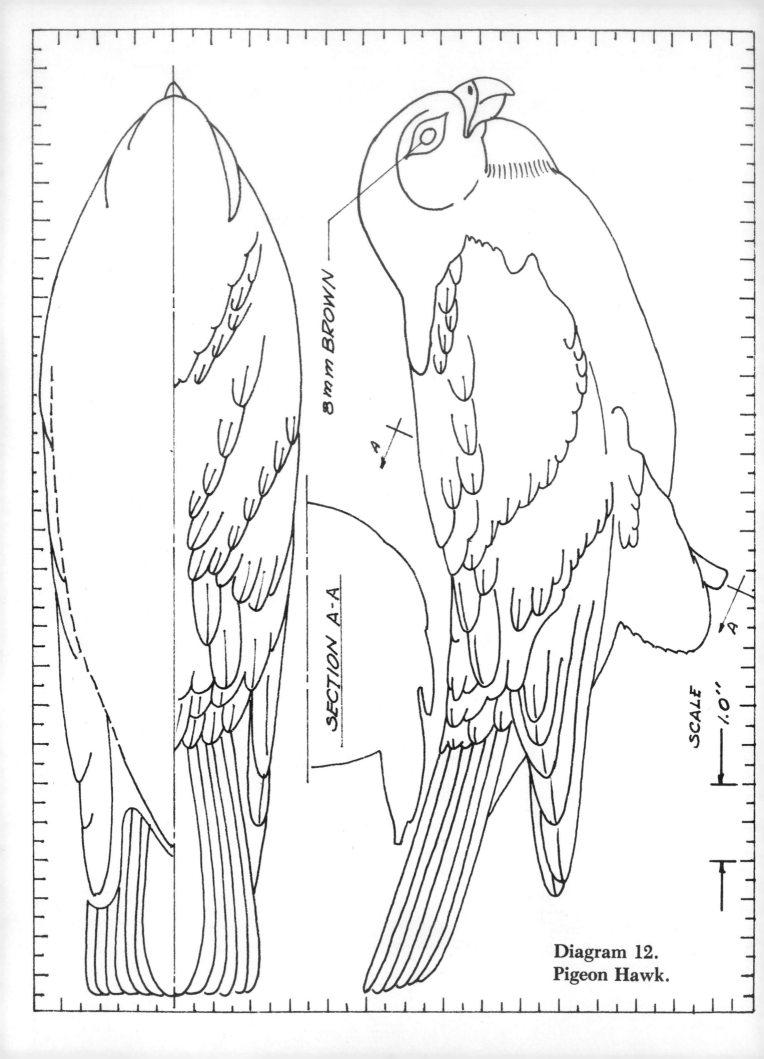

8mm BROWN

SECTION A-A

A

A

SCALE

1.0"

Diagram 12.
Pigeon Hawk.

V. Raptors

Raptors are birds of prey. All the raptors in this book are diurnal. Most raptors take live prey, but some, such as vultures, are scavengers. All have sharp, hooked bills, strong toes, and curved talons that are used skillfully during the acquisition and consumption of prey. The sexes are usually alike in coloration (the Sparrow Hawk is an exception). Females generally are larger than males.

Pigeon Hawk

This falcon derives its name from its posture and style of flight, which at times resemble that of a pigeon. The similarity to the docile namesake ends there, however, for the Pigeon Hawk (*Falco columbarius*) is a most aggressive predator who will often badger larger birds, including crows and the Great Horned Owl. The Pigeon Hawk's diet consists of small birds and mammals and large insects, especially dragonflies, grasshoppers, and butterflies, which are sometimes consumed kite-like on the wing. This falcon perches high on a rock or tree limb to keep a constant lookout for likely prey. Once sighted, the prey is pursued with the rapid, powerful flight made possible by the pointed wings and long tail typical of falcons. As is the case for most predators, the female Pigeon Hawk is larger than the male.

A pattern for carving a Pigeon Hawk is shown in Diagram 12, which is drawn to a scale eighty percent of life size. To make a life-size pattern,

Figure 64.   The Pigeon Hawk.

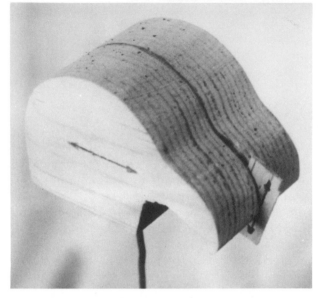

Figure 65.   Typical technique for carving raptors: slot the beak and reinforce it with a thin piece of wood. Arrow indicates the grain of the head block.

Figure 67.   Close-up of the Pigeon Hawk's completed head and beak.

Figure 66.   A perching Pigeon Hawk.

connect the lines at the margins of the drawing and redraw the pattern with the squares method on a grid sheet containing four lines to the inch. It is possible to construct the carving from a single block of wood provided that the grain aligns with the gap formed by the wings and the tail. The beak should be slotted and reinforced (see Figure 65).

Construct the feet and toes from wire (coat-hanger wire will do), using a portion of the method described in Diagram 17 for assembly. Temporarily tape only the middle toe wire to the end of the core wire to be inserted into the bird. Then follow the procedures outlined in Diagram 17 for

Figure 68.   The completed Pigeon Hawk carving.

the remaining toes. By using this modified procedure, both the feet and the toes will, when wrapped with thread, have approximately the correct diameters. Talons should be long and curved. The adult male Pigeon Hawk has slate upper parts streaked with black; a white throat;

tawny cheeks, collar, and underparts streaked with brown; and a black barred tail with a white tip. Females and young males are more brownish.

Sparrow Hawk

Because it can be readily trained, the Sparrow Hawk or American Kestrel, as it is sometimes called, has often been the first bird of novice falconers. Not much larger than a Robin, the Sparrow Hawk (*Falco sparverius*) is not only the smallest but to many observers the most colorful of our falcons. The male has slate-blue wings and a russet back and tail. When opened, the wings and tail display black and white striped and checkered undersides. The female is larger than the male but is similarly marked except for a barred brown back, wings, and tail. Both sexes have two black "eye spots" that give them the appearance of having eyes in the back of their heads.

In the wild the Sparrow Hawk inhabits all but the arctic regions of the Western Hemisphere where domestic tractability, small size, and attractive coloration do not mitigate its raptorial instincts; it is a fierce, aggressive predator that must kill to survive. Despite its name, only a minimum of the prey consists of sparrows and other small birds. The majority of the diet is made up of rodents, which a single bird may consume at a rate of nearly three hundred per year. Usually the unsuspecting prey is spotted on the ground as the bird rides the wind currents aloft, where it seems to hang almost motionless. Plummeting to earth swiftly and silently, the Sparrow Hawk kills its rodent prey instantly with a quick bite from the sharply hooked and notched bill that crushes the base of the rodent's skull.

Of particular note is this bird's amazing eyesight. The eyes are coated with an oily substance that filters out haze and glare. Each retina contains approximately one-and-one-half million visual cells—eight times as many as in the human eye. Thus the Sparrow Hawk can see everything a person can with the aid of an eight-power lens. Even more remarkable is that during the rapid plunge from air to ground to obtain a prey, the bird's eye focus is perfectly synchronized with the rate of descent.

The patterns for carving a male Sparrow Hawk with open wings appear in Diagram 13. To carve a female likeness, the patterns should be increased slightly in size. Use a minimum of four pieces of stock for this carving: one for the body and tail, another for the head, and two for the wings. The pattern indicates that the tail is

Figure 69.   The Sparrow Hawk.

Figure 70.   *Undersides of Sparrow Hawk wings. Note the two different shapes, which reflect the bird's orientation to the wind.*

Figure 73.   *Top sides of the wings, body, and feet of the Sparrow Hawk.*

Figure 71.   *The tree branch is parallel to the curved right wing on the sheltered side of the bird.*

Figure 74.   *The bird's straight left wing is braced against the wind.*

Figure 72.   *Feather detailing with a pyroelectric pen.*

Figure 75.   *Inserting a wing into its body slot.*

closed, but if you wish to make an open tail, you will need a fifth piece of stock of sufficient length and width. A three-fourths-inch-thick piece of clear pine shelving board works well for this purpose, as, indeed, it may for each wing.

When a single block of wood is used for the wings, as was the case for both the Sparrow Hawk and Bald Eagle carvings in this book, each wing carving will be essentially a two-sided relief. The problem is that as you complete the feathers, it is easy for the knife or chisel to break through from one side to the other. In addition much of the carving is against the grain, thus the flight feathers are easily broken when they are separated. To prevent this occurrence, the cross section of the wings must be thicker, and they will lack the proper amount of feather separation.

To avoid these problems, you may make each feather separately with the grain properly aligned and then assemble all the feathers together to form a wing. This technique will eliminate the cross-grain carving problems, but it too has drawbacks. Each feather must have the right curvature in order for it to correspond properly with those adjacent to it, and the final assembly requires a combination of dexterity, correctly contoured slots for each feather, and jigs or fixtures. I don't recommend one method over the other, but do suggest both be tried to establish your choice.

Two separate wing patterns are provided (Diagrams 13C and 13D). Both patterns were used for the carving in the photographs. You may wish to make your carving in this manner, or you may use just one pattern for both wings. Which option to follow depends on how your carving is to be mounted. One wing (Diagram 13C) is straight as if braced against updrafts and wind currents, the other (Diagram 13D) is bent between primaries and secondaries as if sheltered and not subject to such forces (see Figures 70 and 73). The tree branch in the photographs is parallel to the right wing (sheltered side); the left wing (unsheltered side) is braced against the wind (see Figures 71 and 74).

All components—tail feather, wings, and so forth—should be carved and barbs indicated with a pyroelectric pen as much as possible before final assembly. The procedures for carving the bill and making the feet are the same as those described for the Pigeon Hawk.

The depicted bird is of course in a perching attitude even though both wings are open. You may want to change the patterns to show a bird in flight. Photographs will help you orient the bird in various flight phases such as take-off, acceleration, soaring, deceleration, and landing. Once you have decided how to create any of these wing positions, you will need to invent a mounting device that is in keeping with the bird's activity. Some possible methods include securing feet to tree limbs for birds taking off and landing, and attaching wings or tails to ground objects such as reeds for birds that are accelerating.

Soaring birds are perhaps the most difficult to mount and sometimes may look as if they never left their perch, or, when suspended, look as though they were mated with the proverbial "sky hook." Raptors can be attached to carved prey but the danger here is that the bird will appear grotesquely carnivorous. You may derive additional ideas for natural, structurally adequate mounting devices from displays of stuffed birds at museums and galleries.

Figure 77. Another view of the partially "burned" Sparrow Hawk carving.

Figure 76. The mounted Sparrow Hawk carving, feather detailing with a pyroelectric pen only partially completed.

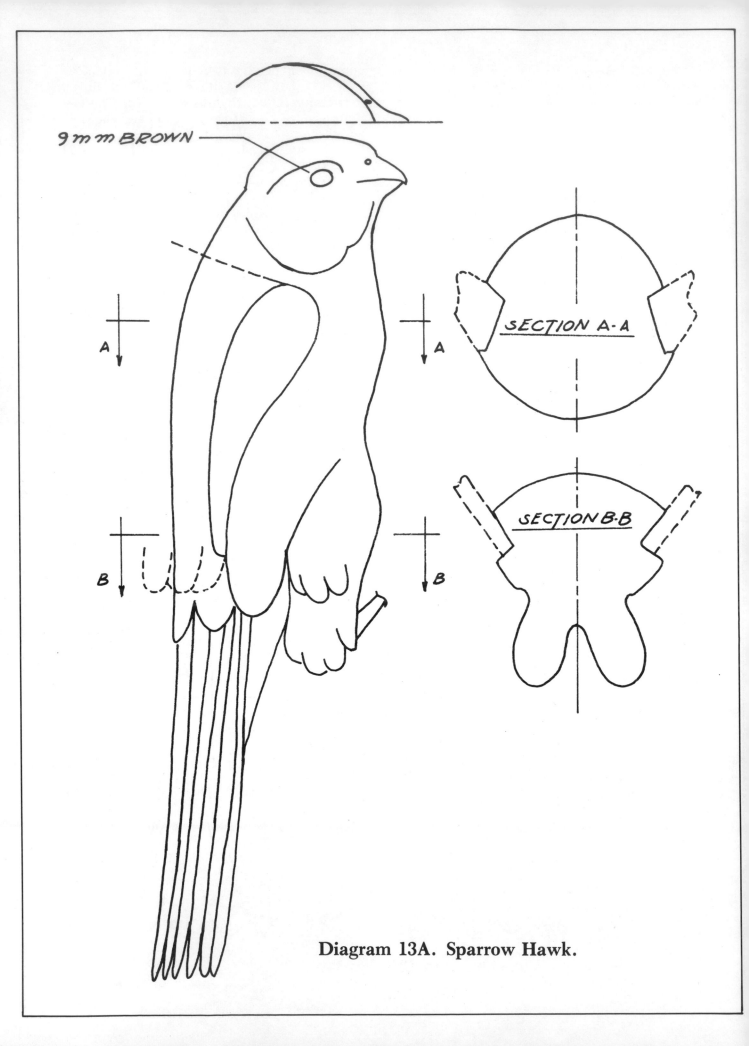

9 m m BROWN

SECTION A-A

SECTION B-B

Diagram 13A. Sparrow Hawk.

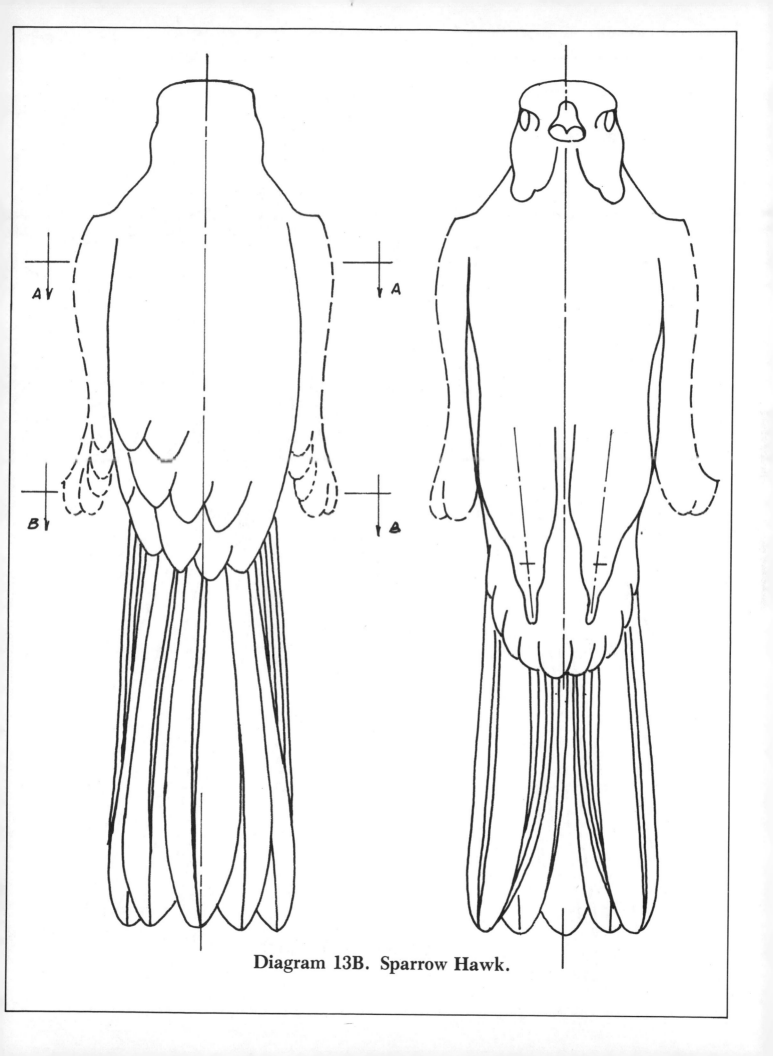

Diagram 13B. Sparrow Hawk.

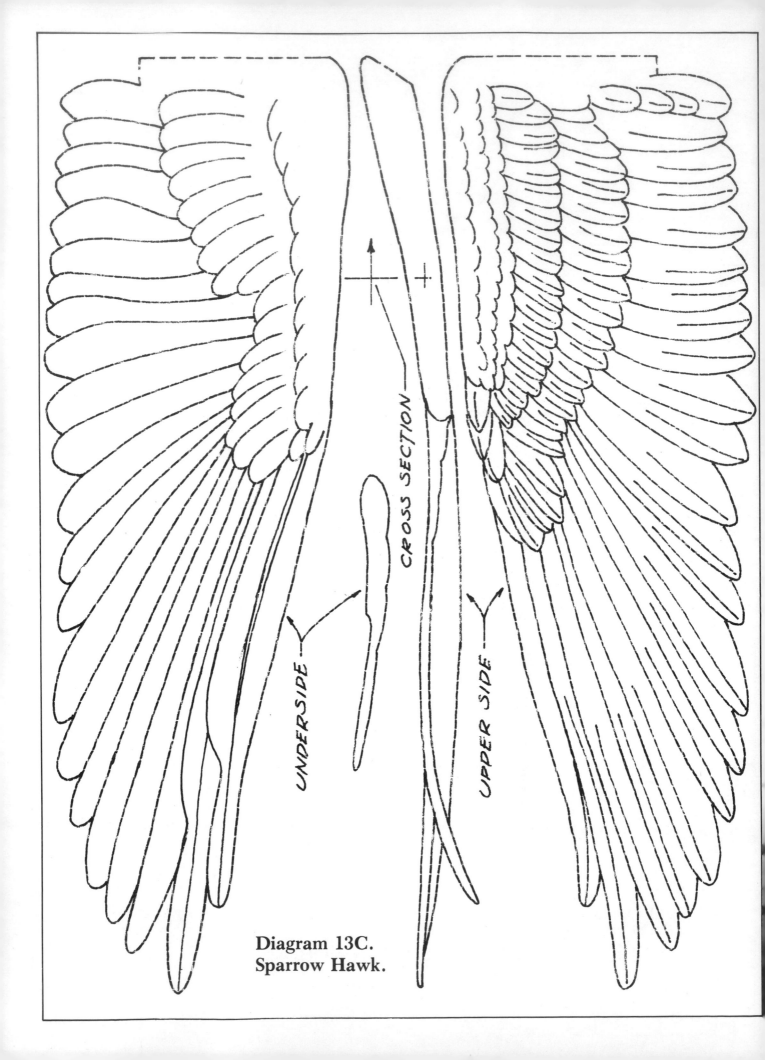

CROSS SECTION

UNDERSIDE

UPPER SIDE

Diagram 13C.
Sparrow Hawk.

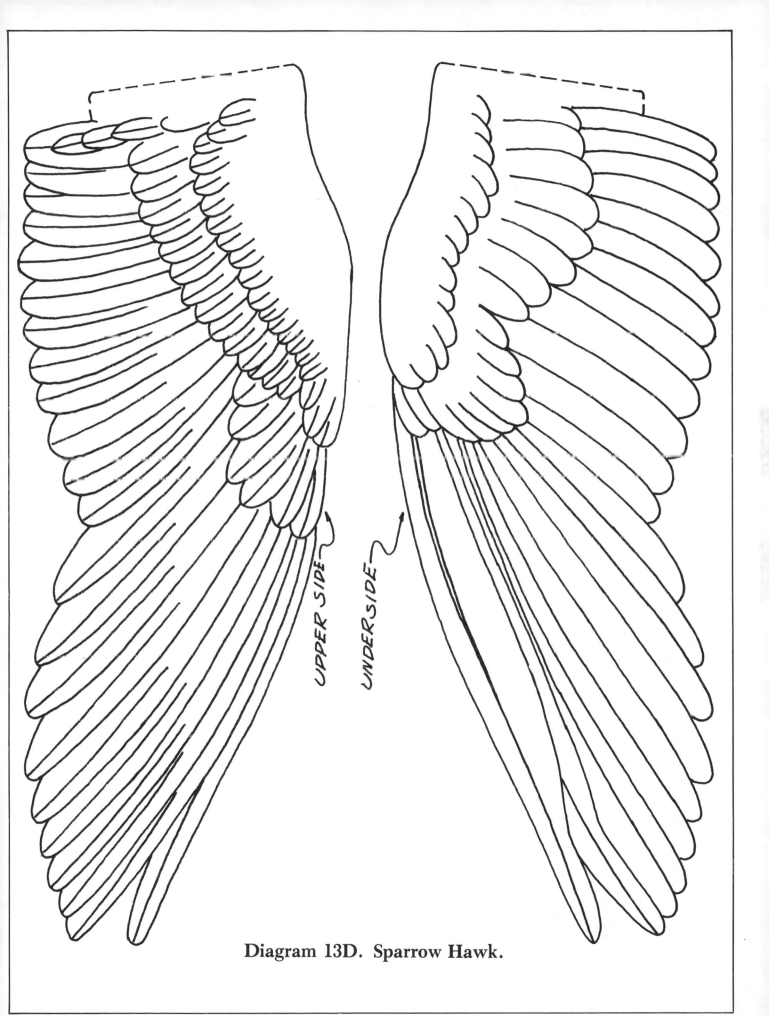

UPPER SIDE

UNDERSIDE

Diagram 13D. Sparrow Hawk.

Bald Eagle

The eagle has long been a symbol of strength and courage. It went into battle with the Persian hosts and its likeness rode on the standards of Roman legions. So, appropriately, the Bald Eagle (*Haliaeetus leucocephalus*), found only on the American continent, was chosen by Congress in 1782 to be the national emblem even though Ben Franklin would have much preferred the Wild Turkey.

Because of its dependence on fish for its diet, the Bald Eagle usually lives near water, particularly large rivers, lakes, and the sea. Unfortunately its numbers in recent years have decreased to a point where today it is found almost only on the Alaska, Florida, and Texas coasts. The Bald Eagle's huge, bulky nest is built primarily of sticks and is usually located in a fork high in a tree. The nest is added to year after year and ultimately may reach twenty feet in depth and

nine feet in diameter. Once the two white eggs are laid, both parents share nest duties. The young are able to fly in about thirteen weeks; their plumage is black and brown. It is not until they reach the age of four to five years that they acquire the adult white head and tail on a brown body.

Two separate Bald Eagle carving patterns—one with closed wings, the other with open wings—are provided in Diagrams 14 and 15 respectively. These patterns were drawn approximately one-fourth life size. The adult bird can measure up to three feet from beak to tail and nearly seven feet in wing span. The size of the patterns can of course be changed rather easily by means of the squares method; a scale reference (hash marks) has been indicated in the margins of the patterns for this purpose. Before increasing the size of a pattern, however, first consider such factors as the size and availability of the stock, the tools (such as a band saw) that

Figure 78.   The perching Bald Eagle carving.

Figure 79.   Close-up of the head and beak of a perching Bald Eagle.

will be required, and, possibly most important, where the finished carving is to be displayed. Both of the depicted carvings were scaled to half of life size, which seemed to work well for the closed-wing bird, but makes the open-wing version require a large display area. Perhaps the pattern's scale of one-fourth might have been a better choice.

For the open-wing carving, use a one-inch piece of shelving board for the wings if the bird is carved to the scale of the pattern. A single piece of stock is adequate for both body and tail. For the closed-wing bird, use two pieces of stock with the grain running parallel to the tail for the body. Hollow out each piece a bit as described earlier for the Laughing Gull project. Use a third piece of stock for the head.

The body for the depicted half-scale open-wing carving was also made from two pieces of stock that had been hollowed out and then glued together. The tail was made from a separate piece

of stock that was inserted into the body. Since much of the Bald Eagle's feet is covered with feathers, two additional blocks were inserted into slots in the body for the foot feathers.

The wings were made from two blocks of wood, each measuring 3″ × 9″ × 21″, and cut on a band saw. The length was a bit more than that required by the pattern, but it proved useful at the inboard section of the wing as a handle inserted into a vice during wing shaping and carving. Once each wing was completed, the excess stock was trimmed to match the body slots.

The finished carving was mounted on a one-fourth-inch-diameter steel rod bent to correspond to the underside of the tail feathers and then inserted into the body. The stand was made from leftover pieces of wing stock. Feet for both the closed- and the open-wing birds can be made by using the five-wire technique (Diagram 16) or by carving a wooden dowel (Diagram 21), depending on the scale chosen for the carving.

Figure 80. Perching Bald Eagle seen from the rear.

Figure 81. The perching Bald Eagle on its stand.

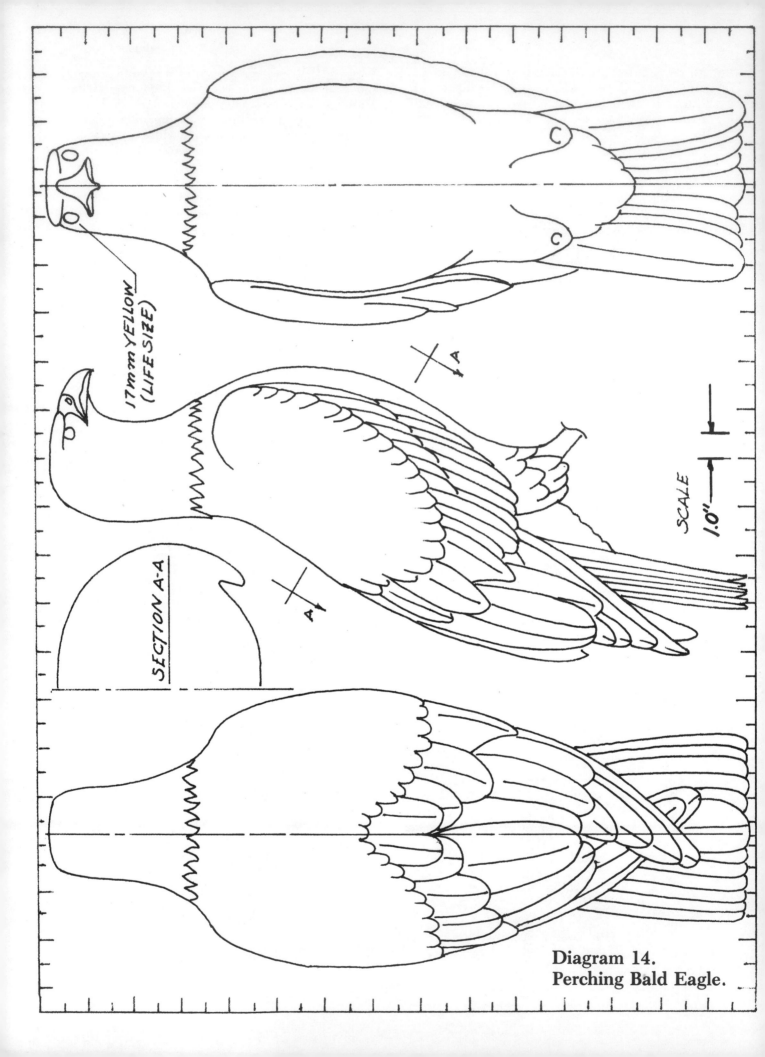

17mm YELLOW (LIFE SIZE)

SECTION A-A

A

A

SCALE 1.0"

Diagram 14.
Perching Bald Eagle.

Figure 82. *The mounted open-wing Bald Eagle.*

Figure 84. *Close-up of the head, body, and feet of the open-wing Bald Eagle.*

Figure 85. *Rear view of the open-wing carving showing the wing span.*

Figure 83. *The open-wing Bald Eagle carving.*

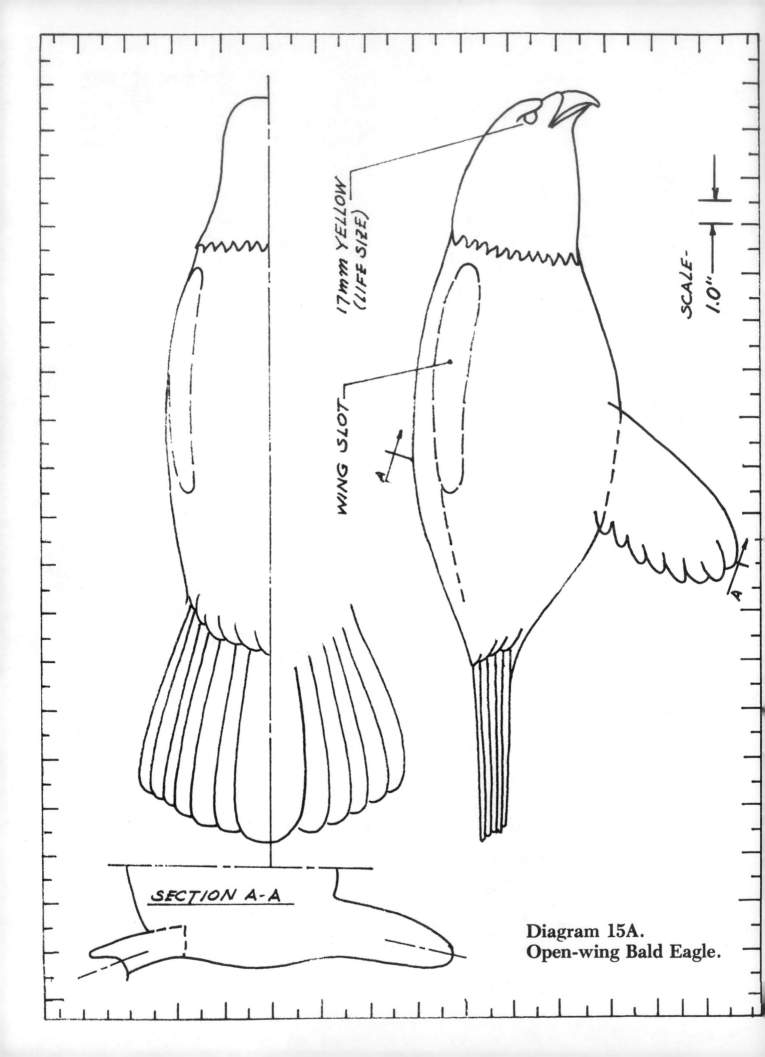

17mm YELLOW
(LIFE SIZE)

WING SLOT

SCALE—
1.0"

A

A

SECTION A-A

Diagram 15A.
Open-wing Bald Eagle.

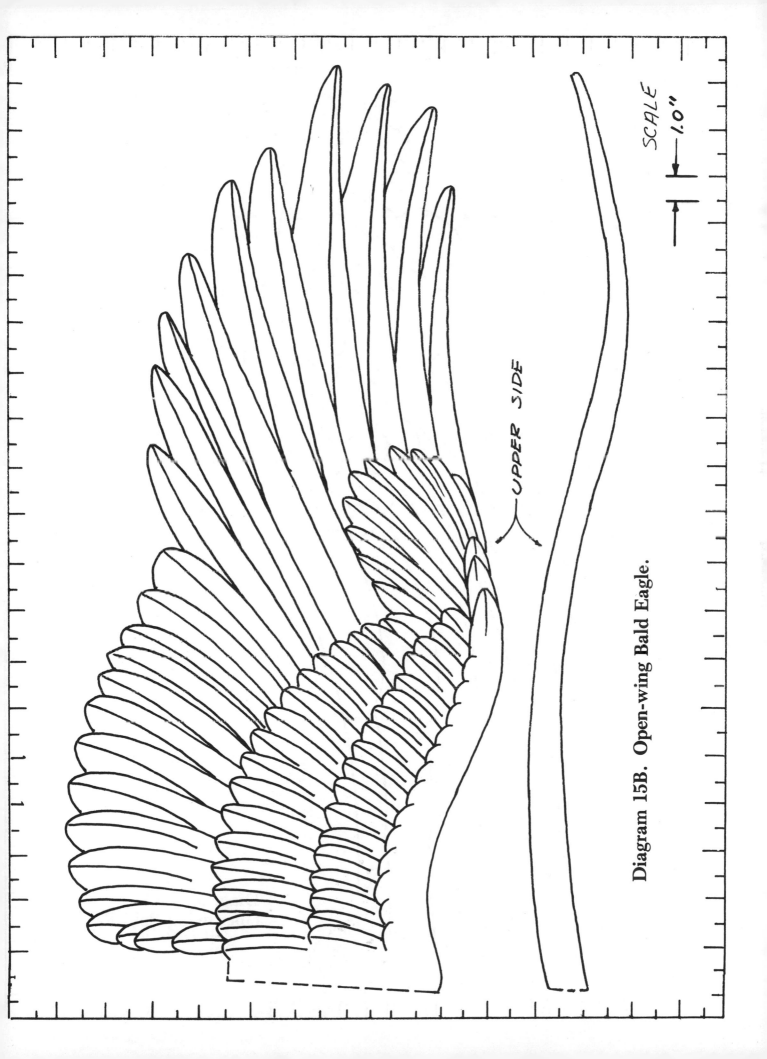

UPPER SIDE

SCALE
|← 1.0" →|

Diagram 15B. Open-wing Bald Eagle.

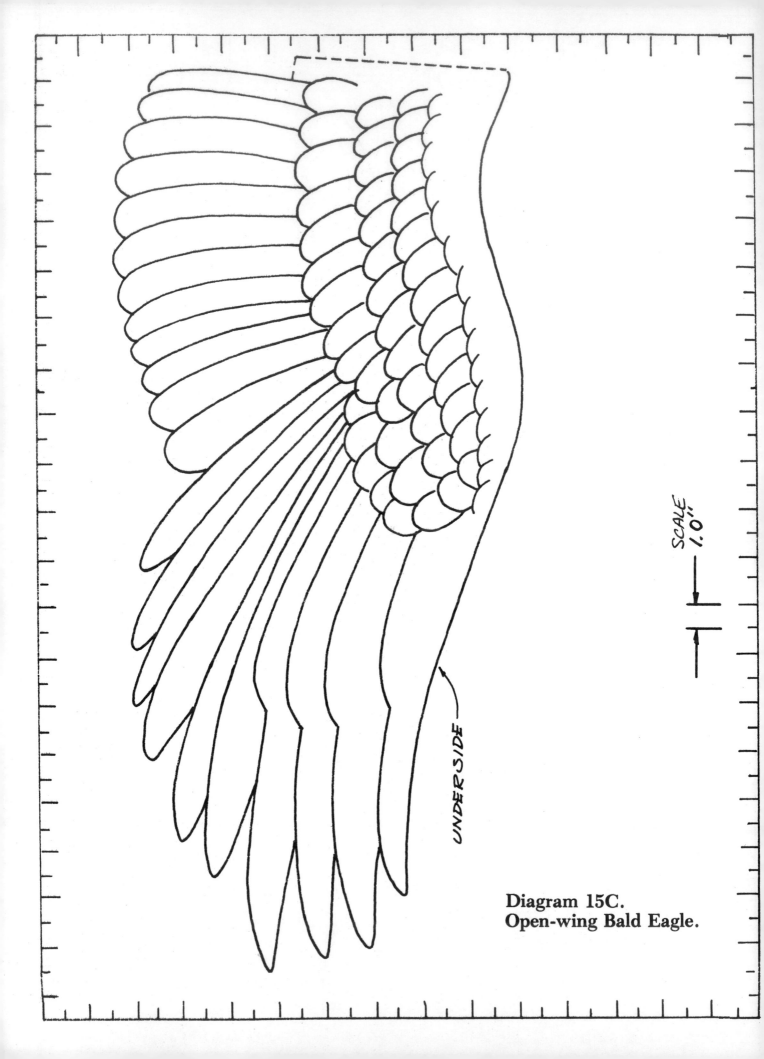

UNDERSIDE

SCALE
1.0"

Diagram 15C.
Open-wing Bald Eagle.

Appendix: Feet for Carved Birds

The feet, especially, distinguish a good carving from one not quite so good. If the feet do not look realistic, neither does the bird.

Ideally the feet, like the bird, should be made from wood, and this is possible for larger birds. For smaller birds the diameter of the feet is something less than that of a round toothpick. In addition to being difficult to carve, such feet would not provide sufficient structural support to the bird and could be easily broken. Combinations of wire and string offer an easier and more practical solution and can be made to look quite realistic.

Suggested methods for making feet for the birds in this book are shown in Diagrams 16–21. The first two methods for medium and small birds were originally included in *Carving Realistic Birds* and are reprinted here for your convenience. The other methods are for plovers, gulls, quail, and large raptors.

The core wire for these feet should always be strong and resilient. You might use piano wire or steel rod, depending on diameter requirements. Wire for the toes can often be a softer and more pliable material such as fine copper or aluminum wire, opened paper clips, or coat hangers. All wire should first be cut to the approximate length and each end ground to a point before assembly. Nylon sewing thread is recommended for winding feet and toes. Once wound, the entire assembly should be dipped into sanding sealer to fill in gaps and bond all strands. In lieu of tape, super glue can be used to hold the wire strands together. When using these glues, make sure that your thumb and forefinger are not pressed together over an area containing the glue as they will quickly become stuck together and be very difficult to separate. While your creative efforts may be okay, you may not wish to express this fact permanently by sign language.

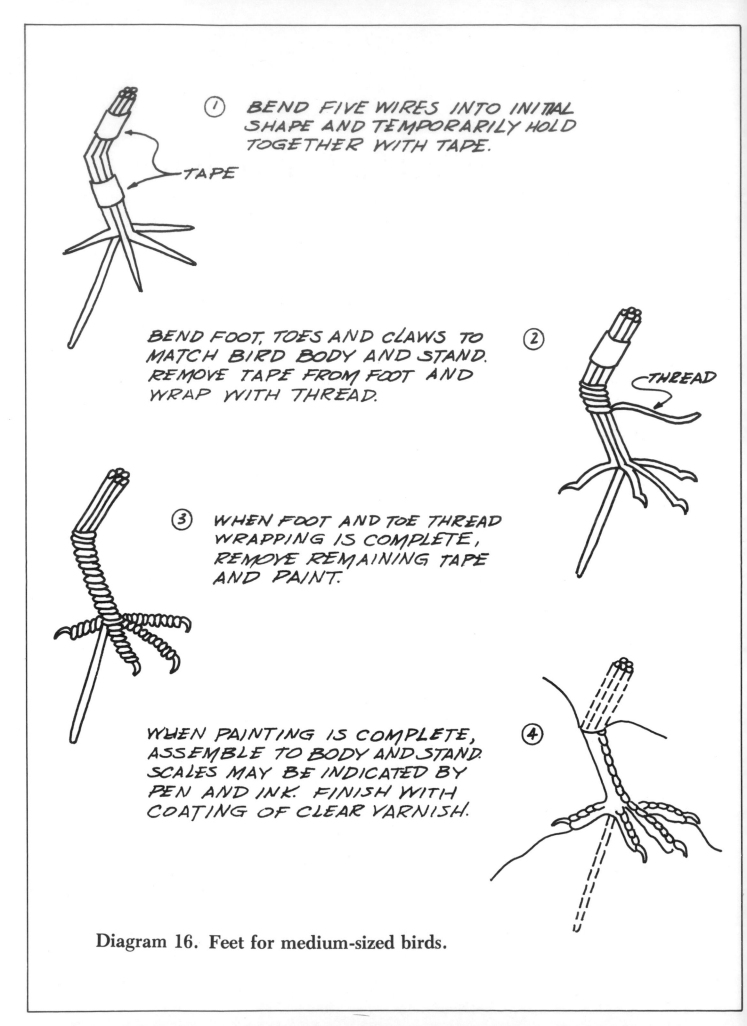

① BEND FIVE WIRES INTO INITIAL SHAPE AND TEMPORARILY HOLD TOGETHER WITH TAPE.

TAPE

BEND FOOT, TOES AND CLAWS TO MATCH BIRD BODY AND STAND. REMOVE TAPE FROM FOOT AND WRAP WITH THREAD.

② THREAD

③ WHEN FOOT AND TOE THREAD WRAPPING IS COMPLETE, REMOVE REMAINING TAPE AND PAINT.

WHEN PAINTING IS COMPLETE, ASSEMBLE TO BODY AND STAND. SCALES MAY BE INDICATED BY PEN AND INK. FINISH WITH COATING OF CLEAR VARNISH.

④

Diagram 16. Feet for medium-sized birds.

① BEND FIVE WIRES INTO INITIAL SHAPE AND HOLD TOGETHER WITH TAPE.

BEND TOES, CLAWS AND FOOT TO MATCH BIRD BODY AND STAND. LEAVE TAPE AND WRAP ALL SURFACES EXCEPT CLAWS WITH THREAD.

②

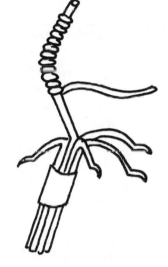

③ WITH THREAD WRAPPING COMPLETE, PAINT AND ASSEMBLE TO BIRD BODY AND STAND.

Diagram 17. Feet for small birds.

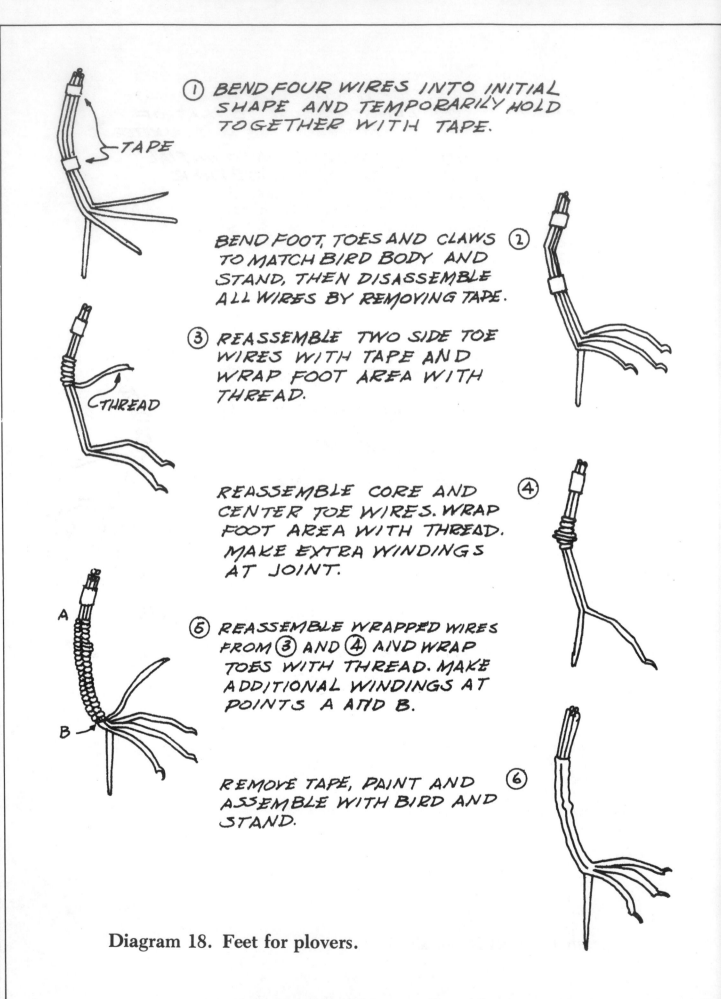

① BEND FOUR WIRES INTO INITIAL SHAPE AND TEMPORARILY HOLD TOGETHER WITH TAPE.

TAPE

② BEND FOOT, TOES AND CLAWS TO MATCH BIRD BODY AND STAND, THEN DISASSEMBLE ALL WIRES BY REMOVING TAPE.

③ REASSEMBLE TWO SIDE TOE WIRES WITH TAPE AND WRAP FOOT AREA WITH THREAD.

THREAD

④ REASSEMBLE CORE AND CENTER TOE WIRES. WRAP FOOT AREA WITH THREAD. MAKE EXTRA WINDINGS AT JOINT.

⑤ REASSEMBLE WRAPPED WIRES FROM ③ AND ④ AND WRAP TOES WITH THREAD. MAKE ADDITIONAL WINDINGS AT POINTS A AND B.

A

B

⑥ REMOVE TAPE, PAINT AND ASSEMBLE WITH BIRD AND STAND.

Diagram 18. Feet for plovers.

① DRILL A SMALL LONGITUDINAL HOLE THROUGH THE CENTER OF A PIECE OF WOOD STOCK WHICH HAS BEEN CUT TO A LENGTH EQUAL TO THAT OF THE BIRD'S FOOT. INCREASE THE HOLE DIAMETER AT ONE END OF THE STOCK TO A DEPTH EQUAL TO APPROXIMATELY 1/4 OF STOCK LENGTH.

② INSERT A PIECE OF WIRE THROUGH THE HOLE AND PROTRUDING AT BOTH ENDS OF THE STOCK BY APPROXIMATELY 3 INCHES. BEND 3 ADDITIONAL WIRES 90° FOR TOES AND INSERT THEM INTO THE LARGER HOLE.

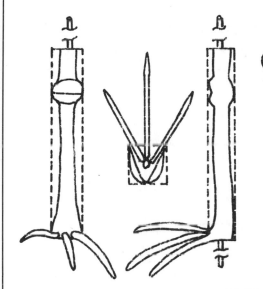

③ SHAPE STOCK AS SHOWN AND BEND 3 TOE WIRES TO MATCH THE STAND. CUT AND BEND AS NEEDED THE CORE WIRE TO MATCH HOLES DRILLED INTO THE BIRD'S BODY AND THE SAND.

④ CARVE THE BACK OF THE FOOT TO INDICATE THE EXISTENCE OF A TOE. WRAP FORWARD TOES WITH THREAD, THEN BEND AND GLUE A PIECE OF WOOD VENEER TO THE BOTTOM OF THESE TOES FOR WEBBING.

⑤ INDICATE FOOT SCALES WITH A SMALL FILE. PAINT APPROPRIATE COLOR AND ASSEMBLE TO BIRD AND STAND.

Diagram 19. Feet for gulls.

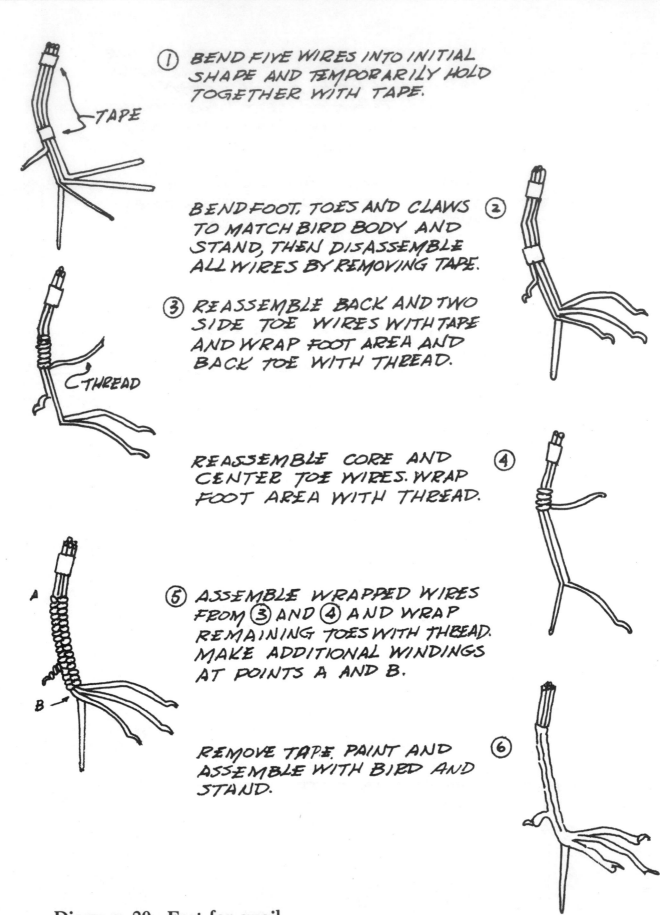

① BEND FIVE WIRES INTO INITIAL SHAPE AND TEMPORARILY HOLD TOGETHER WITH TAPE.

TAPE

② BEND FOOT, TOES AND CLAWS TO MATCH BIRD BODY AND STAND, THEN DISASSEMBLE ALL WIRES BY REMOVING TAPE.

③ REASSEMBLE BACK AND TWO SIDE TOE WIRES WITH TAPE AND WRAP FOOT AREA AND BACK TOE WITH THREAD.

THREAD

④ REASSEMBLE CORE AND CENTER TOE WIRES. WRAP FOOT AREA WITH THREAD.

A

B

⑤ ASSEMBLE WRAPPED WIRES FROM ③ AND ④ AND WRAP REMAINING TOES WITH THREAD. MAKE ADDITIONAL WINDINGS AT POINTS A AND B.

⑥ REMOVE TAPE. PAINT AND ASSEMBLE WITH BIRD AND STAND.

Diagram 20. Feet for quail.

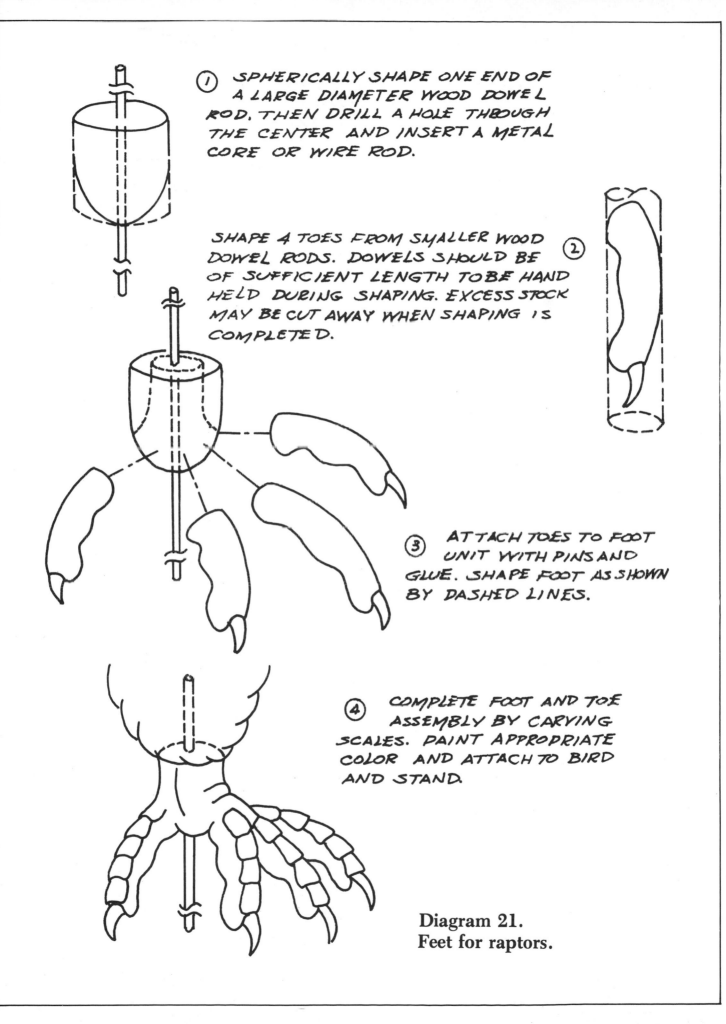

1. SPHERICALLY SHAPE ONE END OF A LARGE DIAMETER WOOD DOWEL ROD. THEN DRILL A HOLE THROUGH THE CENTER AND INSERT A METAL CORE OR WIRE ROD.

2. SHAPE 4 TOES FROM SMALLER WOOD DOWEL RODS. DOWELS SHOULD BE OF SUFFICIENT LENGTH TO BE HAND HELD DURING SHAPING. EXCESS STOCK MAY BE CUT AWAY WHEN SHAPING IS COMPLETED.

3. ATTACH TOES TO FOOT UNIT WITH PINS AND GLUE. SHAPE FOOT AS SHOWN BY DASHED LINES.

4. COMPLETE FOOT AND TOE ASSEMBLY BY CARVING SCALES. PAINT APPROPRIATE COLOR AND ATTACH TO BIRD AND STAND.

Diagram 21.
Feet for raptors.